# Conquer KS3 Chemistry with CGP!

OK, so there's a whole lot to learn in KS3 Chemistry — everything from elements and reactions to volcanoes and recycling.

Helpfully, this brilliant CGP book chops the whole lot up into bite-sized tests. They're perfect for finding out which bits you're already ace at, and which bits still need some work. Plus there are tricky mixed tests to keep you on your toes.

And at the back of the book, you'll find full answers and a progress chart so you can keep track of how you're doing. You'll be a Chemistry expert in a flash!

# CGP — still the best ☺

Our sole aim here at CGP is to produce the highest quality books — carefully written, immaculately presented and dangerously close to being funny.

Then we work our socks off to get them out to you — at the cheapest possible prices.

# Contents

## Classifying Materials

| | |
|---|---|
| Test 1 | 2 |
| Test 2 | 4 |
| Test 3 | 6 |
| Test 4 | 8 |
| Test 5 | 10 |
| Test 6 | 12 |
| Test 7 | 14 |
| Test 8 | 16 |
| Test 9 | 18 |
| Test 10 | 20 |

## Chemical Changes

| | |
|---|---|
| Test 1 | 22 |
| Test 2 | 24 |
| Test 3 | 26 |
| Test 4 | 28 |
| Test 5 | 30 |
| Test 6 | 32 |
| Test 7 | 34 |
| Test 8 | 36 |

## The Earth and the Atmosphere

| | |
|---|---|
| Test 1 | 38 |
| Test 2 | 40 |
| Test 3 | 42 |
| Test 4 | 44 |
| Test 5 | 46 |
| Test 6 | 48 |

## Mixed Questions

Test 1 .................................................................................................................. 50
Test 2 .................................................................................................................. 52
Test 3 .................................................................................................................. 54
Test 4 .................................................................................................................. 56
Test 5 .................................................................................................................. 58
Test 6 .................................................................................................................. 60

Answers ............................................................................................................... 62
Progress Charts ................................................................................................... 70

Published by CGP

Editors: Emma Clayton, Georgina Fairclough, Paul Jordin

With thanks to Barrie Crowther and Emily Forsberg for the proofreading.
With thanks to Emily Smith for the copyright research.

ISBN: 978 1 78908 580 8

Printed by Elanders Ltd, Newcastle upon Tyne.
Clipart from Corel®
Illustrations by: Sandy Gardner Artist, email sandy@sandygardner.co.uk

Based on the classic CGP style created by Richard Parsons.

Text, design, layout and original illustrations © Coordination Group Publications Ltd. (CGP) 2020
All rights reserved.

Photocopying this book is not permitted, even if you have a CLA licence.
Extra copies are available from CGP with next day delivery • 0800 1712 712 • www.cgpbooks.co.uk

Classifying Materials

# Test 1: States of Matter

Give yourself **10 minutes** to do this test — there are **6 questions** to answer.

**Quick-fire Question**

1. Which diagram shows the particle arrangement for a gas?
   Circle your answer.

   (A) ~circled~   B   C

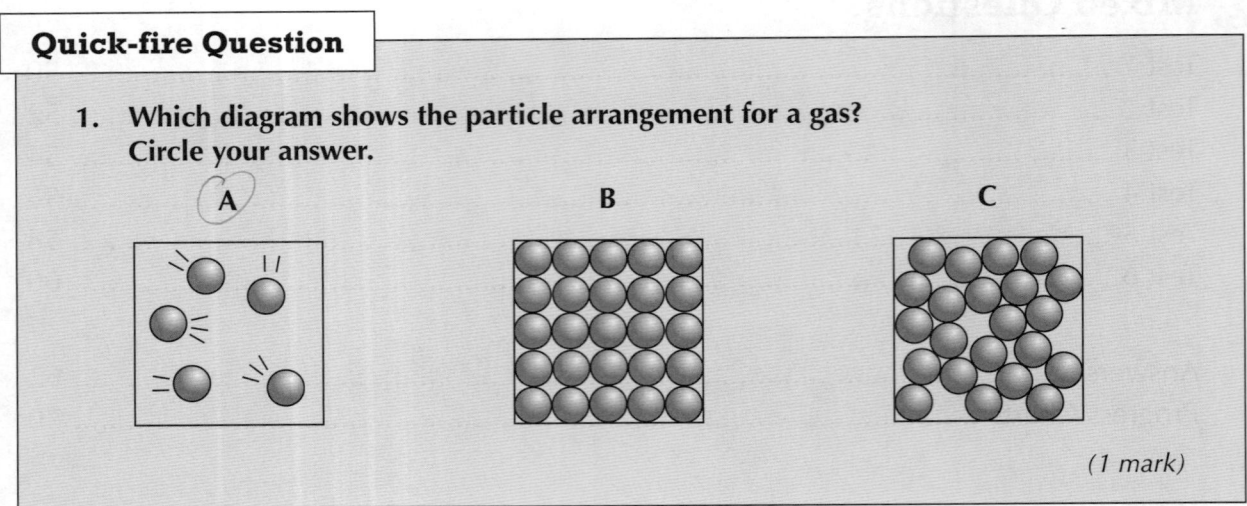

*(1 mark)*

2. Complete the table below.

| | Solid | Liquid | Gas |
|---|---|---|---|
| Density | ~low~ high | medium | low |
| Compressibility | not easily squashed | can't | can't |

*(2 marks)*

3. Complete the sentences below using some of the words given in the box.

   | irregular   strong   vibrate   fast   fixed   weak   regular   rotate |

   There are ......strong...... forces of attraction between particles in a solid.

   The particles are held in a very ......fixed (regular)...... arrangement.

   They ......vibrate...... to and fro in ......fixed...... positions.

   *(2 marks)*

4. **Complete the sentences below by circling the correct words in the brackets.**

   In diffusion, particles move from an area of ( **higher** / ~~lower~~ )

   concentration to an area of ( **higher** / ~~lower~~ ) concentration.

   *(1 mark)*

5. **Decide whether each of the sentences below is true or false. Tick the correct box.**

   |  | True | False |
   |---|---|---|
   | A change of state is a physical change. | ✓ | |
   | A change of state involves a change in mass. | | ✓ |
   | A change of state involves a change in heat energy. | ✓ | |

   *(2 marks)*

6. **Below is the heating graph of a substance. Write the correct letter in each space below to match the labels to the correct parts of the graph.**

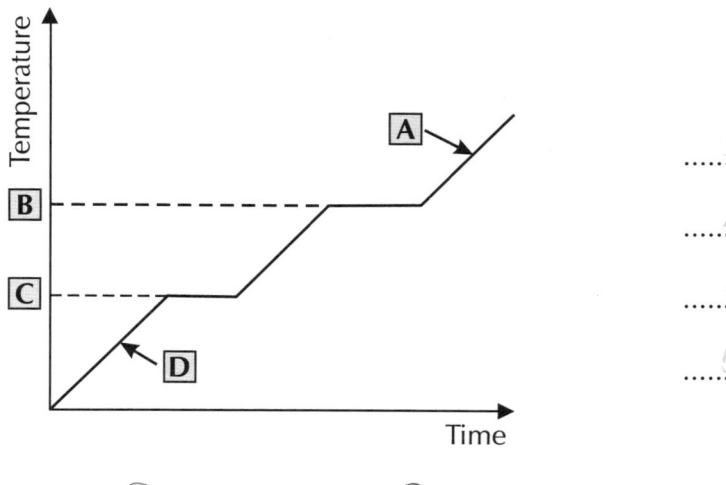

   ....D..... solid

   ....A..... gas

   ....C..... boiling point

   ....B..... melting point

   *(2 marks)*

Score: /10

# Test 2: States of Matter

Give yourself **10 minutes** to do this test — there are **6 questions** to answer.

**Quick-fire Question**

1. Water can be a solid, a liquid or a gas. Which two of the following properties have an effect on the state of matter of water? Circle the correct answers below.

   A   Mass

   B   Temperature

   C   Pressure

   D   Time

   *(1 mark)*

2. Draw lines to match up the words with the correct definitions.

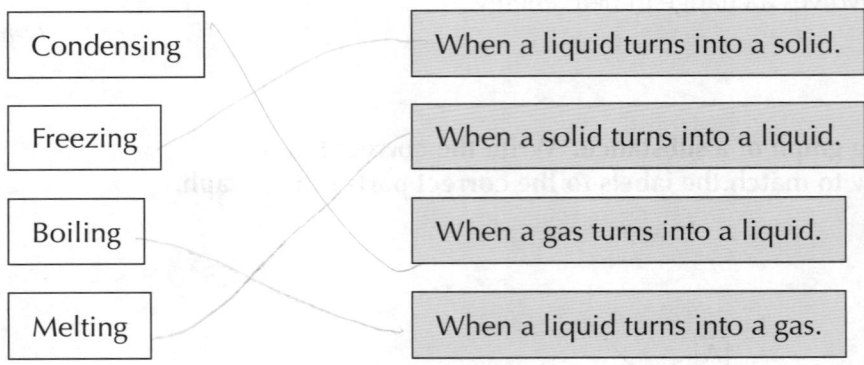

   *(1 mark)*

3. Complete the sentences below by circling the correct words in the brackets.

   When a substance is heated, its particles ( **gain** / **lose** ) energy.

   This makes the particles move more ( **quickly** / **slowly** ),

   which ( **strengthens** / **weakens** ) the forces of attraction between the particles.

   *(2 marks)*

Classifying Materials: Test 2

4. **Decide which state(s) of matter each statement below is describing. Tick the correct boxes.**

|  | solids | liquids | gases |
|---|---|---|---|
| Have a definite volume. | ✓ | ☐ | ☐ |
| Match the shape of the container. | ☐ | ✓ | ☐ |
| Flow easily. | ☐ | ✓ | ☐ |

*(2 marks)*

5. **Complete the sentences below using some of the words given in the box.**

| reacting | increases | volume | temperature |
|---|---|---|---|
| slower | reduces | harder | colliding |

Gas pressure is caused by gas particles ...*colliding*... with the inner walls of the container. Increasing the ...*temperature*... makes the particles move faster. This means they hit the walls ...*harder*... and more often. This ...*increases*... the pressure.

*(2 marks)*

6. **Horatio sits on a beach ball. The gas inside the beach ball is compressed. Why can gases be easily compressed?**

...The particles are not in a fixed arrangement so there's a lot of space...

*(2 marks)*

Score: /10

# Test 3: States of Matter

Give yourself **10 minutes** to do this test — there are **6 questions** to answer.

**Quick-fire Question**

1. In which state of matter does diffusion occur the fastest?
   Circle the correct answer below.

   A   Solids          B   Liquids          **C**   Gases

   *(1 mark)*

2. How could you increase the pressure of a gas in a sealed container?
   Tick two boxes.

   ☑ Increase the temperature         ☐ Increase the volume

   ☐ Decrease the temperature         ☐ Decrease the volume

   *(1 mark)*

3. Complete the description for each of the states of matter shown below by circling the correct words in the brackets.

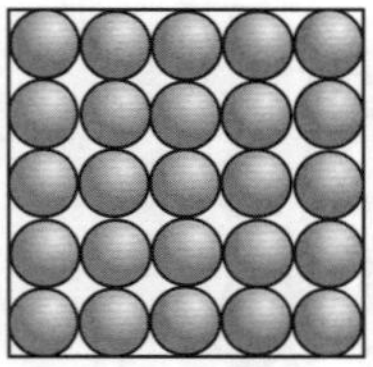

   ( Can / **Cannot** )          Particles are              ( **Strong** / Weak )
   be easily                    ( **free to move** /        forces of attraction
   compressed.                   fixed in position ) .      between particles.

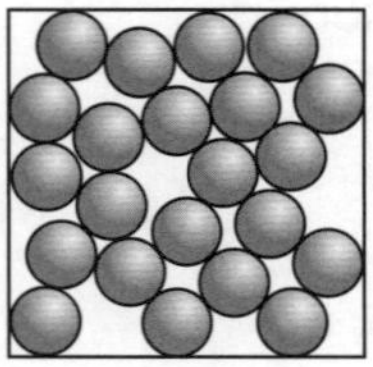

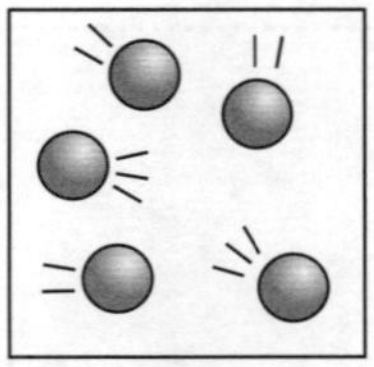

   *(2 marks)*

4. What is it called when a solid turns into a gas?

   ...................................................................................................................................

   *(1 mark)*

5. **Sketch a cooling curve for water on the axes below. Label the different parts of the curve with the correct states of matter and the names of the processes as the water changes state.**

*(3 marks)*

6. **Complete the sentences below using some of the words given in the box.**

| increases    decreases    pressure    volume    air particles |

When a balloon full of air is squeezed, the ......*volume*...... of the

balloon decreases. This means that the ......*air particles*...... inside the balloon

are squashed into a smaller space. The smaller the space becomes,

the more the pressure ......*increases*...... . The balloon will eventually pop

if the ......*pressure*...... increases too much.

*(2 marks)*

**Score:** /10

# Test 4: Atoms, Elements and Compounds

Give yourself **10 minutes** to do this test — there are **6 questions** to answer.

**Quick-fire Question**

1. Which of the following are NOT correct symbols for elements?
   Circle your answers.

   A (cU)    B  Al    C  (MG)    D  H₂O

   E  C     F  Fe    G  (ox)    H  Na

   *(1 mark)*

2. Complete the sentences below using some of the words given in the box.

   | ~~compounds~~ | element | gases | mixture | ~~many~~ | four | atoms |

   All matter is made up of ......atoms....... .

   There are ......*missing*...... types of atom.

   Each ......element...... contains only one type of atom.

   All ......compounds...... contain at least two types of atom bonded together.

   *(2 marks)*

3. Fill in the gaps in the table below.

   | Compound | Formula |
   |---|---|
   | water | H₂O |
   | Carbon dioxide | CO₂ |
   | sodium hydroxide | H₂SO₄ |
   | Sodium chloride | NaCl₂ |

   *(2 marks)*

Classifying Materials: Test 4

4. Complete the sentences below about chemical reactions.
   Circle the correct words in the brackets.

   The chemicals you start with are called ( **reactants** / **products** ).

   The chemicals you end up with are called ( **reactants** / **products** ).

   *(1 mark)*

5. Below is a blank periodic table. Shade and label the positions of:

   A  The transition metals     B  The noble gases     C  Group 1

   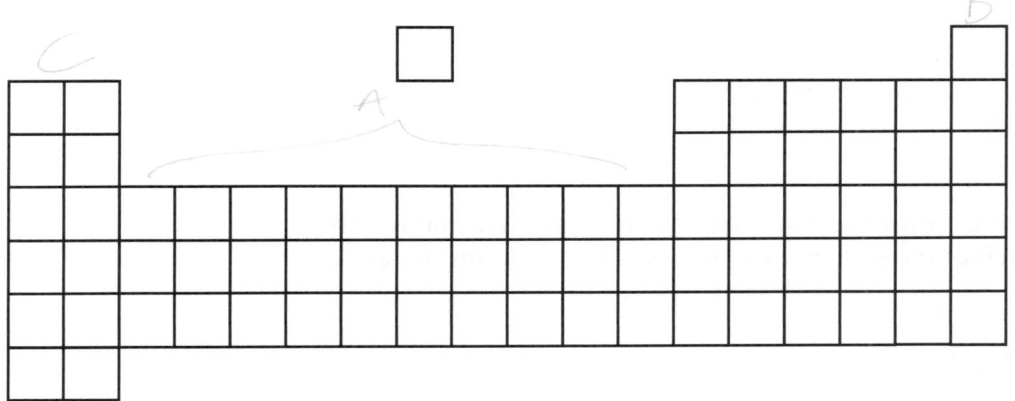

   *(2 marks)*

6. A compound has the chemical formula $C_5H_5FO_2$.
   Complete the table by writing down the name of each element
   in the compound and the number of atoms of each element.

   | Element | Number of atoms |
   |---|---|
   | carbon | 8 |
   | hydrogen | 1 |
   | fluorine | 9 |
   | oxygen | 17 |

   *(2 marks)*

   Score: /10

# Test 5: Atoms, Elements and Compounds

Give yourself **10 minutes** to do this test — there are **7 questions** to answer.

**Quick-fire Question**

1. A compound contains magnesium, carbon and oxygen atoms only. Which of the following could be the name of the compound? Circle your answer.

    A  Carbon manganate

    B  Magnesium oxide

    C  Magnesium carbonate

    D  Carbon chloride

    *(1 mark)*

2. The Group 1 elements are shown below. Decide whether each of the sentences is true or false. Tick the correct box.

    Group 1

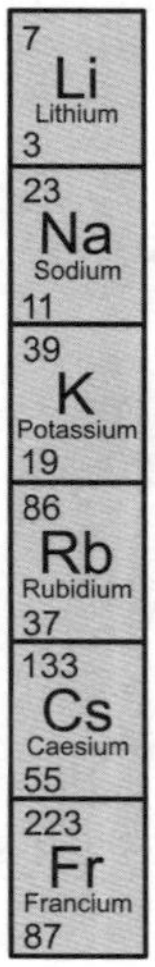

    |  | True | False |
    |---|---|---|
    | The elements in Group 1 are all metals. | ✓ | |
    | Group 1 elements are more reactive than Group 0 elements. | ✓ | |
    | Sodium is more reactive than caesium. | ✓ | |
    | All the Group 1 elements react with water. | | |
    | Potassium is more reactive than lithium. | | ✓ |

    *(2 marks)*

3. What is an element?

    ...........................................................................................................................

    *(1 mark)*

Classifying Materials: Test 5

4. Draw lines to match up the symbol to the correct element.

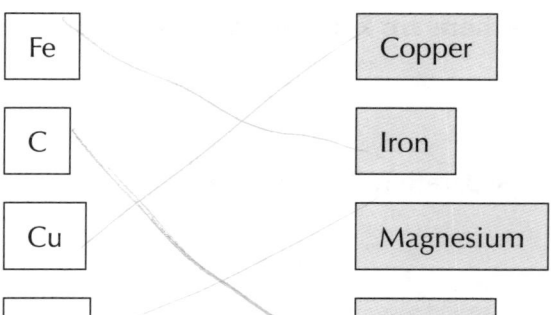

(1 mark)

5. Air consists mostly of nitrogen gas, $N_2$, and oxygen gas, $O_2$. Explain why air is not classed as a compound.

...Nitrogen and oxygen are not bonded so air is a mixture...

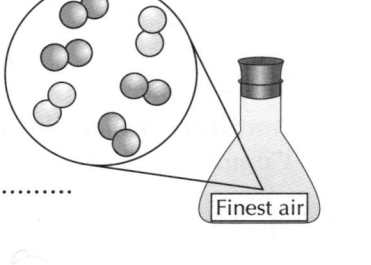

(1 mark)

6. Label each of the following as an element, compound or mixture.

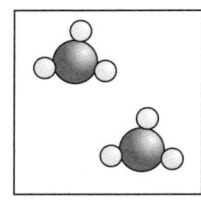 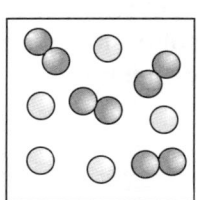 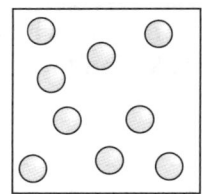 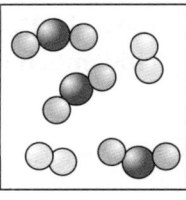

A — compound   B — mixture   C — element   D — mixture

(2 marks)

7. Complete the word and balanced symbol equations for this chemical reaction.

sodium + chlorine ⟶ sodium ...chloride...

2 ...Na... + $Cl_2$ ⟶ 2 ...NaCl...

(2 marks)

Score: /10

# Test 6: Mixtures

Give yourself **10 minutes** to do this test — there are **7 questions** to answer.

**Quick-fire Question**

1. Which of these methods could you use to separate water from ink? Circle your answer.

    A  Melting

    B  Filtration

    C  (Simple distillation)

    *(1 mark)*

2. A mixture is made by adding a soluble substance and an insoluble substance to water. Complete the sentences below by circling the correct words in the brackets.

    The insoluble substance can be removed from the mixture by ( evaporation / (filtration) ).

    The soluble substance can be separated from the water by ( (evaporation) / filtration ).

    *(1 mark)*

3. A beaker containing water weighs 100 g. 40 g of salt is stirred into the water but only 35 g of the salt dissolves before the solution becomes saturated. How much does the beaker and its contents weigh now?

    ............................ 140g ............................

    *(1 mark)*

4. The diagram shows a chromatogram. Which dye (A, B or C) is the most soluble in the solvent used in the experiment? Tick the correct box.

    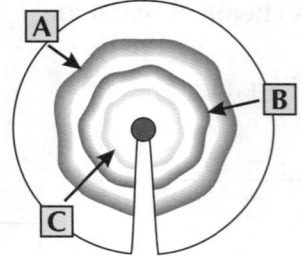
    ☐ A   ☐ B   ☑ C

    *(1 mark)*

Classifying Materials: Test 6

5. **Draw lines to match each term with its definition.**

| Term | Definition |
|---|---|
| Solute | A mixture of a solute and a solvent. |
| Solution | Will not dissolve. |
| Saturated | A solution where no more solid will dissolve at that temperature. |
| Solubility | The solid being dissolved. |
| Insoluble | A measure of how much solute will dissolve. |

Matches drawn:
- Solute → The solid being dissolved.
- Solution → A mixture of a solute and a solvent.
- Saturated → A solution where no more solid will dissolve at that temperature.
- Solubility → A measure of how much solute will dissolve.
- Insoluble → Will not dissolve.

*(3 marks)*

6. **Decide whether each of the sentences below is true or false. Tick the correct box.**

|  | True | False |
|---|---|---|
| A pure substance can be made up of one type of compound. | ✓ |  |
| The molecules in pure substances can be separated using physical methods. |  | ✓ |
| Air is a mixture of different gases. | ✓ |  |
| A mixture contains different substances which aren't chemically combined. | ✓ |  |

*(2 marks)*

7. **Under standard lab conditions, the boiling point of a sample of water is found to be 102 °C. What can you say about the purity of the water?**

...........................................................................................................................................................

*(1 mark)*

Score: ___ / 10

# Test 7: Mixtures

Give yourself **10 minutes** to do this test — there are **8 questions** to answer.

**Quick-fire Question**

1. How could you make more salt dissolve in a saturated solution of salt?
   Circle the correct answer below.

   A   Add more salt.

   B   Increase the temperature.

   C   Pour away some of the solution.

   *(1 mark)*

2. Rock salt is a mixture of sand and salt.
   Put the following steps for the separation of rock salt in order, from 1-4.

   ☐ The mixture is filtered with a funnel and filter paper.

   ☐ The rock salt is added to water and stirred until the salt has dissolved.

   ☐ The mixture is heated until the water has evaporated.

   ☐ The rock salt is ground up with a pestle and mortar.

   *(2 marks)*

3. Some oil is added to a sample of water. The oil doesn't dissolve, even after stirring. What word can be used to describe the oil?

   ...................................................................................................................................................

   *(1 mark)*

4. A student has a beaker of sea water. She wants to separate out the mixture to obtain salt and pure water. Suggest why heating the sea water in an evaporating dish isn't a suitable method for this.

   ...................................................................................................................................................

   ...................................................................................................................................................

   *(1 mark)*

5. Complete the sentences below using the words given in the box.
   Each word is used once.

   | solute | solvent | solution | dissolving | bonds |
   |---|---|---|---|---|

   When you add a solute to a ..................., the ................... holding the solute

   particles together sometimes break. The ................... particles then mix with the

   particles in the liquid forming a ................... . This is called ................... .

   *(2 marks)*

6. Fractional distillation is used to separate a mixture of three liquids. Liquid A is collected first, then liquid B, then finally liquid C. Which liquid has the highest boiling point? Tick the correct box.

   ☐ Liquid A

   ☐ Liquid B

   ☐ Liquid C

   *(1 mark)*

7. What name is given to the pattern of spots or rings formed on a piece of filter paper during a chromatography experiment?

   ...................................................................................................................

   *(1 mark)*

8. Which of the following pieces of equipment are needed for a chromatography experiment? Tick all the boxes that apply.

   ☐ Condenser  ☐ Beaker  ☐ Filter paper  ☐ Thermometer

   ☐ Solvent  ☐ Bunsen burner  ☐ Funnel  ☐ Pestle and mortar

   *(1 mark)*

   Score: ☐ /10

# Test 8: Mixtures

Give yourself **10 minutes** to do this test — there are **6 questions** to answer.

**Quick-fire Question**

1. Which of these methods is NOT useful for separating out mixtures?
   Circle the correct answer.

   A  Distillation

   B  Oxidation

   C  Evaporation

   D  Filtration

   *(1 mark)*

2. Put the following steps for a chromatography experiment in order, from 1-7.
   The first one has been done for you.

   [ ] Put the paper into a beaker containing a small amount of solvent.

   [ ] Remove the paper from the solvent.

   [ ] Roll up the paper.

   [ ] Unroll the paper.

   [ ] Put spots of ink along the pencil line.

   [1] Draw a pencil line near the bottom of a piece of chromatography paper.

   [ ] Wait for the solvent to seep up the paper.

   *(3 marks)*

3. A sugar cube is dissolved into a cup of water. What is formed during this process?
   Tick all the boxes that apply.

   [ ] a compound       [ ] a mixture         [ ] a solvent

   [ ] a solution       [ ] a pure substance  [ ] a solute

   *(1 mark)*

Classifying Materials: Test 8

4. The image shows some ink samples (A-D) that have been separated out by chromatography. Which two samples contain the same dye?

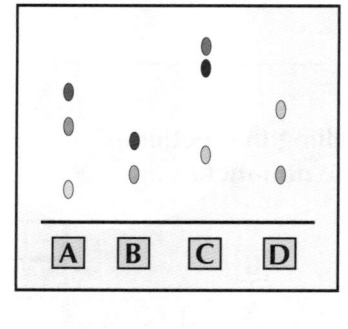

.......... and ..........

*(1 mark)*

5. Complete the sentences below using some of the words given in the box.

| heated | cooled | complex | fractional | highest | lowest |

In ........................ distillation, a flask containing different liquids is ........................

and the liquid that boils at the ........................ temperature evaporates first.

The vapour is then ........................ until it condenses and is collected.

*(2 marks)*

6. The diagram below shows the simple distillation of an ink and water mixture. Write labels for each letter in the space provided.

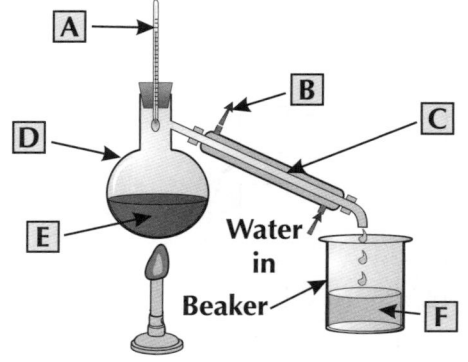

A: ........................................
B: ........................................
C: ........................................
D: ........................................
E: ........................................
F: ........................................

*(2 marks)*

Score: /10

# Test 9: Properties of Materials

Give yourself **10 minutes** to do this test — there are **6 questions** to answer.

**Quick-fire Question**

1. Circle the letter that is labelling the section of the periodic table where the non-metals are.

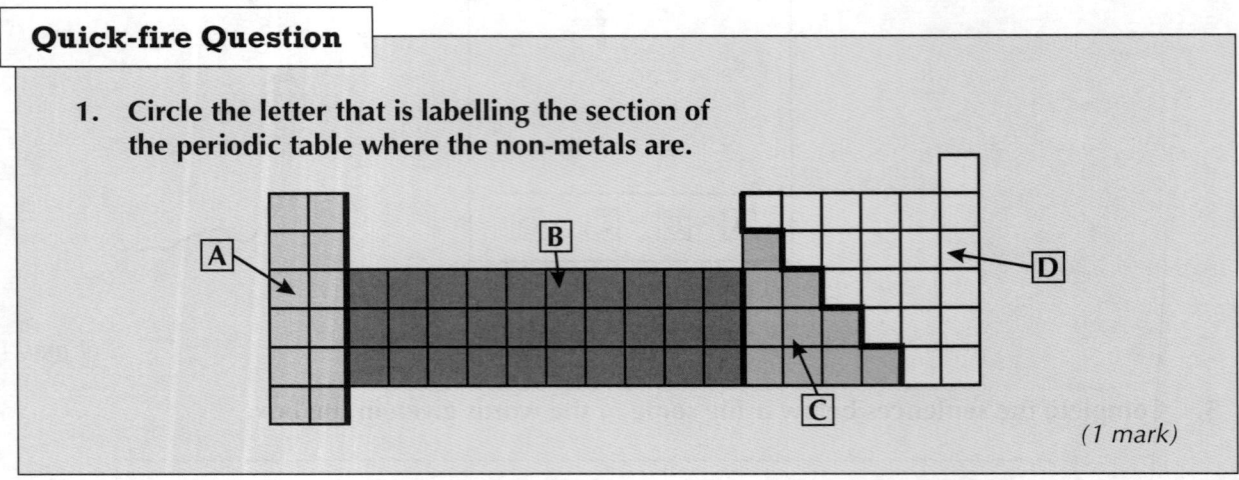

*(1 mark)*

2. Complete the sentences below by circling the correct words in the brackets.

    A material that contains a combination of metals is called ( **an alloy** / **a composite** ).

    Adding ( **iron** / **oxygen** ) to a material will make it magnetic.

    *(1 mark)*

3. Decide whether each of the following are typical properties of metals or non-metals. Tick the correct box.

| | Metals | Non-metals |
|---|---|---|
| brittle and can shatter easily | ☐ | ☐ |
| have high densities | ☐ | ☐ |
| good insulators of electricity | ☐ | ☐ |
| poor conductors of heat | ☐ | ☐ |
| high melting and boiling points | ☐ | ☐ |
| shiny when polished | ☐ | ☐ |

*(2 marks)*

Classifying Materials: Test 9

4. The particles in metals are very close together.
   Explain why this makes metals good conductors of heat.

   ..................................................................................................................................

   ..................................................................................................................................
   *(1 mark)*

5. Draw lines to match up the materials with an appropriate description.

   | Polymers |     | Materials made up of two or more materials together. |
   
   | Ceramics |     | Stiff and brittle materials made by baking substances like clay. |
   
   | Composites |   | Substances made up of long chains of molecules. |
   
   *(1 mark)*

6. Timothée is cooking up a pot of onion soup. Explain why his pot is made from metal, but the pot handles are made from plastic.

   ..................................................................................................................................

   ..................................................................................................................................

   ..................................................................................................................................

   ..................................................................................................................................

   ..................................................................................................................................
   *(4 marks)*

Score: /10

# Test 10: Properties of Materials

Give yourself **10 minutes** to do this test — there are **6 questions** to answer.

**Quick-fire Question**

1. Which of these elements would you expect to have the lowest melting point? Circle the correct answer.

   A  Aluminium
   
   B  Silver
   
   C  Chlorine
   
   D  Zinc

   *(1 mark)*

2. Decide whether each of the sentences below is true or false. Tick the correct box.

   |  | True | False |
   |---|---|---|
   | All metals are magnetic. | ☐ | ☐ |
   | All non-metals are non-magnetic. | ☐ | ☐ |
   | Electrical wires are made of metal. | ☐ | ☐ |
   | All non-metals are gases. | ☐ | ☐ |

   *(2 marks)*

3. Draw lines to match up the properties of metals with their definitions.

   | | |
   |---|---|
   | High tensile strength | Can be drawn into a wire. |
   | Malleable | Can be pulled hard without breaking. |
   | Ductile | Easily shaped. |
   | Sonorous | Makes a sound when hit. |

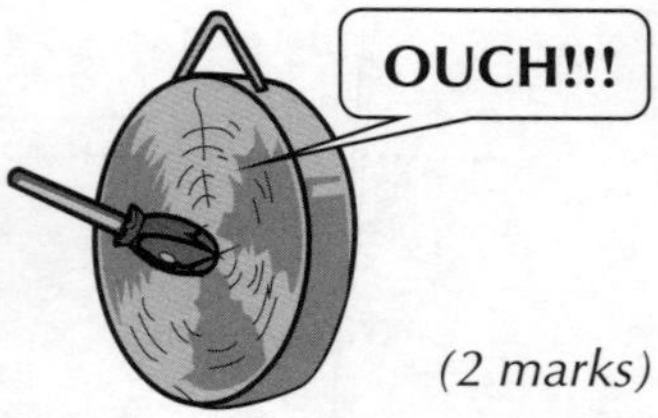

   OUCH!!!

   *(2 marks)*

Classifying Materials: Test 10

4. Which of these properties of graphite make it useful for making pencils?
   Tick the correct box.

   ☐ Graphite conducts electricity well.

   ☐ Graphite conducts heat well.

   ☐ Graphite isn't hard-wearing, so its particles are easily scrubbed away.

   ☐ Graphite is brittle, so it can shatter easily.

   *(1 mark)*

5. What is the name of the free particles that allow metals to conduct electricity?

   .................................................................................................................
   *(1 mark)*

6. Decide whether each of the properties below belongs to polymers, ceramics or both.
   Put each property into the correct column of the table below.

   | can be flexible | electrical insulator | always brittle | always stiff | heat insulator |

   | Polymers | Ceramics | Both |
   |----------|----------|------|
   |          |          |      |

   *(3 marks)*

   Score: ☐ / 10

# Chemical Changes

## Test 1: Chemical Reactions

Give yourself **10 minutes** to do this test — there are **6 questions** to answer.

**Quick-fire Question**

1. Circle the correct statement(s) about chemical reactions.

   A  Energy needs to be supplied in order to start a reaction.

   B  In a chemical reaction, the reactant atoms are destroyed.

   C  The mass of the products is always greater than the mass of the reactants.

   D  All chemical reactions involve a change in energy.

   *(1 mark)*

2. Balance the equation shown below.

   $$CH_4 + \ldots\ldots O_2 \rightarrow CO_2 + \ldots\ldots H_2O$$

   *(1 mark)*

3. Complete the sentences below using the options given in the box.

   | given out to | a decrease | taken in from | an increase |

   In an exothermic reaction, energy is ............................................. the surroundings.

   This is usually shown by ............................................. in the temperature of the reaction mixture.

   In an endothermic reaction, energy is ............................................. the surroundings.

   This is usually shown by ............................................. in the temperature of the reaction mixture.

   *(2 marks)*

Chemical Changes: Test 1

4. Draw lines to match each type of reaction to the most suitable description.

| Combustion | When a substance breaks down to form new substances. |
| Decomposition | When a substance combines with oxygen. |
| Oxidation | When a substance burns in the air to release energy. |

*(2 marks)*

5. Which of the following are always needed in order for a combustion reaction to take place? Tick three boxes.

☐ carbon dioxide   ☐ hydrocarbons   ☐ oxygen

☐ fuel   ☐ a catalyst   ☐ heat

☐ light   ☐ nitrogen   ☐ water

*(3 marks)*

6. What is a catalyst?

..................................................................................................................

..................................................................................................................

*(1 mark)*

Score: /10

# Test 2: Chemical Reactions

Give yourself **10 minutes** to do this test — there are **7 questions** to answer.

**Quick-fire Question**

1.  Which of the following could you not use as a fuel in a combustion reaction? Circle your answer.

    A   Petrol

    B   Natural Gas

    C   Oxygen

    D   Oil

    *(1 mark)*

2.  A flask containing calcium carbonate was heated to make the calcium carbonate undergo thermal decomposition. The mass of the flask and its contents were measured before and after the reaction.

    How would you expect the mass to change, if at all, during this experiment?

    | The mass would decrease. | The mass would stay the same. | The mass would increase. |
    |---|---|---|

    *(1 mark)*

3.  Complete the sentences below by circling the correct answer in the brackets.

    Propane is a hydrocarbon. When propane is burned in a good supply of air,

    a ( **combustion** / **decomposition** ) reaction takes place. The reaction gives out energy

    in the form of ( **electricity** / **heat** ), which means it is ( **exothermic** / **endothermic** ).

    The reaction also gives out energy in the form of ( **light** / **oxygen** ).

    *(2 marks)*

4.  Write a word equation to show what happens when iron oxidises.

    ..................................................................................................................................

    *(1 mark)*

Chemical Changes: Test 2

5. **Which of the following are produced when a hydrocarbon burns in air? Tick two boxes.**

   ☐ carbon dioxide     ☐ nitrogen     ☐ oxygen

   ☐ a salt             ☐ water        ☐ hydrogen

   *(2 marks)*

6. **The symbol equation for the reaction between chlorine and potassium bromide is:**

   $$Cl_2 + 2KBr \rightarrow 2KCl + Br_2$$

   How does the equation show that mass is conserved in this reaction?

   ..........................................................................................................................................

   ..........................................................................................................................................

   ..........................................................................................................................................
   *(1 mark)*

7. **Hydrogen peroxide is a liquid that decomposes to form water and oxygen gas.**

   bubbles of oxygen gas — hydrogen peroxide

   **Potassium permanganate can be used as a catalyst for this reaction.**
   **A scientist has two flasks of hydrogen peroxide.**
   **She adds some potassium permanganate to one of the flasks.**

   Suggest one difference that the scientist will observe between the two flasks.
   Explain your answer.

   ..........................................................................................................................................

   ..........................................................................................................................................

   ..........................................................................................................................................
   *(2 marks)*

   Score: ☐ /10

# Test 3: Chemical Reactions

Give yourself **10 minutes** to do this test — there are **8 questions** to answer.

**Quick-fire Question**

1. A reaction occurs between two liquids in a beaker. Which piece(s) of equipment could be used to find out if the reaction is exothermic? Circle your answer(s).

   A   a gas syringe

   B   a mass balance

   C   a thermometer

   D   a stopwatch

   *(1 mark)*

2. Write a word equation for the reaction between sodium and water to produce sodium hydroxide and hydrogen.

   ...........................................................................................................................................
   *(1 mark)*

3. Sports injury packs can be used instead of ice to chill injuries and prevent swelling. They contain substances that undergo a chemical process when the pack is squeezed.

   Suggest whether the chemical process in a sports injury pack is exothermic or endothermic. Explain your answer.

   ...........................................................................................................................................

   ...........................................................................................................................................
   *(1 mark)*

4. How do catalysts speed up reactions? Tick one box.

   ☐ They raise the temperature of the reactants.

   ☐ They lower the minimum amount of energy required for the reaction to happen.

   ☐ They weaken the bonds between the reactant atoms.

   ☐ They remove impurities from the reaction.

   *(1 mark)*

Chemical Changes: Test 3

5. Copper oxide (CuO) reacts with carbon to form copper metal and carbon dioxide. Write a balanced symbol equation for this reaction.

...................................................................................................................................................
*(2 marks)*

6. Salman has two substances, X and Y.
He reacts 8 g of substance X with 32 g of substance Y, using 2 g of a catalyst.
All of the reactants are used up and only one product is formed.

Which row of the table shows the mass of catalyst and mass of product that Salman will have at the end of this reaction?

|   | mass of product (g) | mass of catalyst (g) |
|---|---|---|
| A | 32 | 2 |
| B | 40 | 2 |
| C | 42 | 0 |
| D | 24 | 2 |
| E | 40 | 0 |

*(1 mark)*

7. A chemical company is considering buying catalysts to speed up their reactions. Give two possible disadvantages to the company of using catalysts.

1. ...................................................................................................................................................

2. ...................................................................................................................................................
*(2 marks)*

8. Ada adds a piece of iron to an open flask, then measures the combined mass of the flask and the iron. Later, Ada reweighs the flask and its contents and discovers that the mass has increased. Suggest the type of reaction that has occurred.

...................................................................................................................................................
*(1 mark)*

Score: /10

# Test 4: Acids and Alkalis

Give yourself **10 minutes** to do this test — there are **6 questions** to answer.

**Quick-fire Question**

1. The salt lithium nitrate is produced from a neutralisation reaction. What is the pH of a lithium nitrate solution? Circle your answer.

   A  0     C  9
   
   B  7     D  14

   *(1 mark)*

2. Leo has the three liquids shown below on the left.
   He measures the pH of each liquid and obtains the readings shown below on the right.
   Draw lines to match each liquid to its pH.

   | sodium hydroxide solution | pH 1 |
   | sulfuric acid | pH 7 |
   | pure water | pH 13 |

   *(1 mark)*

3. What is an indicator?

   ........................................................................................................................

   ........................................................................................................................

   *(1 mark)*

4. Complete the sentences below by circling the correct answer in each set of brackets.

   Magda has a solution of potassium hydroxide. This solution is ( **acidic** / **neutral** / **alkaline** ).

   She adds some nitric acid to the solution. Adding the acid makes the pH of

   the solution ( **increase** / **decrease** / **stay the same** ). After she has added the acid,

   the solution contains ( **a salt** / **an indicator** / **nitrogen dioxide** ).

   *(2 marks)*

Chemical Changes: Test 4

5.  Fill in the blanks to complete the table below.

| Indicator | Colour at pH 6 | Colour at pH 14 |
|---|---|---|
| Universal Indicator | yellow | |
| Litmus Paper | | blue |

*(2 marks)*

6.  Bill decides to make a sample of sodium chloride. He uses the method shown below.

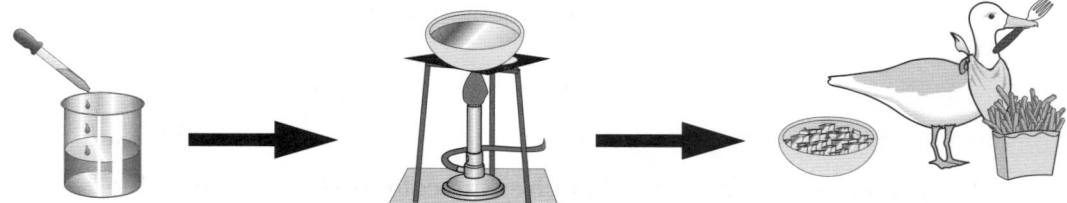

1. Add hydrochloric acid to sodium hydroxide solution.
2. Boil off some of the water.
3. Leave to evaporate until crystals form.

What could Bill do to make sure he doesn't add too much acid in step 1?
How will he know when he's added the right amount of acid?

.................................................................................................................................

.................................................................................................................................

.................................................................................................................................

.................................................................................................................................

*(2 marks)*

Tallulah wants to make a sample of sodium sulfate.
How could she alter Bill's method in order to do this?

.................................................................................................................................

.................................................................................................................................

*(1 mark)*

Score: ☐ /10

# Test 5: Acids and Alkalis

Give yourself **10 minutes** to do this test — there are **7 questions** to answer.

**Quick-fire Question**

1. What type of salt is formed when hydrochloric acid reacts in a neutralisation reaction? Circle your answer.

   A   a chlorate salt      C   a hydride salt

   B   a sulfate salt       D   a chloride salt

   *(1 mark)*

2. Methyl orange is an indicator that gives the colours shown in the table.

   | Colour below pH 4 | Colour above pH 4 |
   |---|---|
   | red | yellow |

   What would you observe if some methyl orange was added to a solution of ammonia?

   ....................................................................................................................................................

   *(1 mark)*

3. What is the general equation for a neutralisation reaction? Tick the correct box.

   ☐ Acid + Alkali → Salt + Water        ☐ Acid + Water → Salt + Alkali

   ☐ Acid + Alkali → Salt + Hydrogen     ☐ Acid + Salt → Alkali + Water

   *(1 mark)*

4. Fill in the gaps to complete the sentences below.

   The pH of the strongest acid is ............ . The pH of the strongest alkali is ............ .

   The pH of a neutral solution is ............ .

   *(3 marks)*

Chemical Changes: Test 5

5.  Jill is evaporating the water in a salt solution. Her apparatus is shown below.
    Fill in the missing labels.

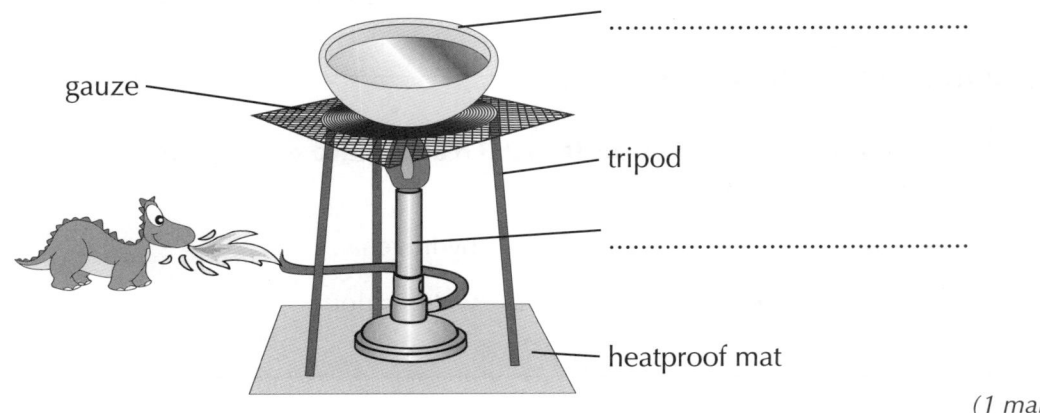

*(1 mark)*

6.  State the type of reaction that occurs when nitric acid is added to potassium hydroxide.
    What is the name of the salt produced in this reaction?

    Type of reaction: ..................................................................................................

    Salt: ..............................................................................................................
    *(2 marks)*

7.  Sonia has two different solutions. She wants to investigate their pH values.
    Give one advantage of using Universal indicator, rather than litmus paper,
    in this investigation.

    ..................................................................................................................

    ..................................................................................................................
    *(1 mark)*

Score: /10

# Test 6: Reactivity and Reactions

Give yourself **10 minutes** to do this test — there are **6 questions** to answer.

**Quick-fire Question**

1. Which gas is produced when a metal reacts with a dilute acid?
   Circle your answer.

   A   oxygen          C   (hydrogen)

   B   carbon dioxide  D   water vapour

   *(1 mark)*

2. Complete the sentences below by circling the correct answer in the brackets.

   Some metals, such as ( **gold** / iron ) are so ( **reactive** / **unreactive** ) that they

   are found in the Earth in their pure form.

   Other metals are mostly found in the Earth as metal ( **oxides** / solutions ) and have

   to be extracted from ( carbon / **ores** ).

   *(2 marks)*

3. Ruby is investigating the displacement reactions of magnesium and iron with different solutions of metal compounds. Put a tick in the box(es) where you'd expect a displacement reaction to take place and a cross where a displacement reaction wouldn't take place. The first row has been done for you.

   |               | zinc sulfate solution, $ZnSO_4$ | potassium chloride solution, $KCl$ | lead nitrate solution, $Pb(NO_3)_2$ |
   |---------------|-----|-----|-----|
   | magnesium, Mg | ✓   | ✗   | ✓   |
   | iron, Fe      | ✗   | ✗   | ✓   |

   *(1 mark)*

Chemical Changes: Test 6

4. Decide whether each of the sentences below is true or false. Tick the correct box.

|  | True | False |
|---|---|---|
| Most soluble non-metal oxides form acidic solutions. | ☐ | ☐ |
| Metals below hydrogen in the reactivity series will react with acids. | ☐ | ☐ |
| Insoluble metal oxides can be used to neutralise acids. | ☐ | ✓ |

*(2 marks)*

5. Put the following elements in order from least reactive to most reactive.

| Carbon | Zinc | Sodium | Hydrogen | Calcium | Copper |

..................................................................................................................................

*(2 marks)*

6. Olivia adds a small piece of magnesium to a test tube containing dilute acid. At the same time, Arvind adds a small piece of iron to a separate test tube containing an equal volume of the same acid. They compare their test tubes side-by-side.

Describe what Olivia and Arvind will observe in this experiment.

..................................................................................................................................

..................................................................................................................................

..................................................................................................................................

*(2 marks)*

Score: ☐ /10

# Test 7: Reactivity and Reactions

Give yourself **10 minutes** to do this test — there are **8 questions** to answer.

**Quick-fire Question**

1. How many products are formed when magnesium reacts with oxygen? Circle your answer.

   **A** One     **C** Three

   **B** Two     **D** Zero — magnesium doesn't react with oxygen.

   *(1 mark)*

2. What is an ore? Tick the correct box.

   ☐ A rock that contains metal or metal compounds.

   ☐ A rock that contains a high percentage of carbon.

   ☐ A rock that contains fossil fuels.

   ☐ A rock that contains acidic compounds.

   *(1 mark)*

3. Sort the metals below by whether or not they can be extracted by reduction with carbon.

   Aluminium    Zinc    Iron    Magnesium

   | Can be extracted using carbon | Can't be extracted using carbon |
   |---|---|
   |  |  |

   *(1 mark)*

4. Metals that can't be extracted from their ores using carbon can be extracted another way.

   Name the method used to extract metals that can't be extracted using carbon.

   ..................................................................................................................................

   *(1 mark)*

Chemical Changes: Test 7

5.  Describe what you could do to determine if a sample of gas in a test tube is hydrogen.

    ..................................................................................................................................

    ..................................................................................................................................

    .................................................................................................................................. *(2 marks)*

6.  Use the information given in the table to put metals X, Y and Z in order from least reactive to most reactive.

    | Metal | Reactivity |
    |---|---|
    | X | Reacts quickly with oxygen if exposed to air. |
    | Y | Displaces metal X from a solution of its salt. |
    | Z | Reacts with oxygen only when heated. |

    .................................................................................................................................. *(1 mark)*

7.  Give two properties of metal oxides.

    1. ................................................................................................................................

    2. ................................................................................................................................ *(2 marks)*

8.  Circle the elements below that form acidic oxides.

    calcium        silicon        nitrogen

    sodium        phosphorus        zinc

    *(1 mark)*

    Score: /10

# Test 8: Reactivity and Reactions

Give yourself **10 minutes** to do this test — there are **6 questions** to answer.

**Quick-fire Question**

1. Which of the following statements about the reactivity series is true?
   Circle your answer.

   A  The lower a metal is in the reactivity series, the more violently it reacts.

   B  In a displacement reaction, a metal higher up the reactivity series can displace a metal lower down the reactivity series.

   C  Metals below carbon in the reactivity series are typically extracted by electrolysis.

   D  Aluminium is above magnesium in the reactivity series.

   *(1 mark)*

2. Sulfur is a non-metal.
   Circle the properties you would expect sulfur dioxide ($SO_2$) to have.

   | gas at room temperature | reacts with alkalis in solution | pH above 7 |

   | neutralises acids | neutral pH | solid at room temperature |

   *(1 mark)*

3. Complete the word equation for the reaction between hydrochloric acid and zinc.

   hydrochloric acid + zinc → .............................. + ..............................

   *(2 marks)*

4. Name a metal that doesn't need to be extracted from an ore.

   ..................................................................................................

   *(1 mark)*

Chemical Changes: Test 8

5.  Complete the sentences below using some of the words from the box.

    | low | tube | acid | oxidises | carbon | oxygen |
    | reduces | high | furnace | neutralises | | |

    Iron is a useful metal that must be extracted from its ore, iron oxide.

    In order to do this, iron oxide is mixed with a fuel called coke and heated to a

    .......................... temperature in a blast .......................... .

    The coke contains .......................... , which ..........................

    the iron oxide to produce iron.
    (2 marks)

6.  Alfie has an iron nail. He places the nail in a test tube containing blue copper nitrate solution. After a while, he notices that the solution has turned green and a brown solid has formed on the nail.

    Suggest the identity of the brown solid.

    ..................................................................................................
    (1 mark)

    Explain Alfie's observations.

    ..................................................................................................

    ..................................................................................................

    ..................................................................................................
    (2 marks)

    Score: /10

# The Earth and the Atmosphere

## Test 1: The Earth's Structure

Give yourself **10 minutes** to do this test — there are **6 questions** to answer.

> **Quick-fire Question**
>
> 1. Which of the elements below do scientists think can be found in the Earth's core? Circle your answer.
>
>    A  nickel           B  copper
>
>    C  sulfur           D  hydrogen
>
>    *(1 mark)*

2. Label the layers of the Earth.

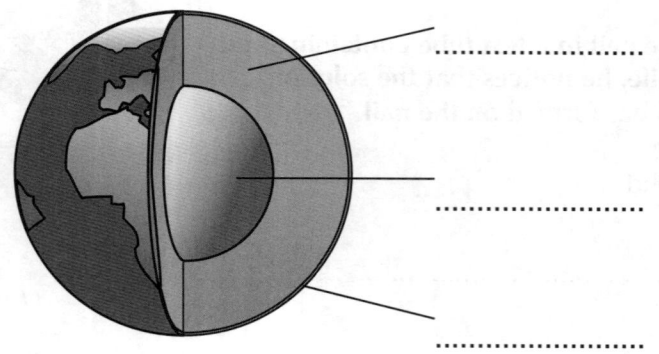
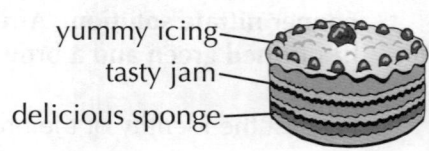

*(1 mark)*

3. Complete the sentences below by circling the correct answers in the brackets.

   The ( **core** / **surface** ) of the planet is broken into several large pieces called

   ( **mantle pieces** / **tectonic plates** ), which move around very ( **slowly** / **quickly** ).

   ( **Volcanoes** / **Hurricanes** ) can occur where two of the pieces meet.

   *(2 marks)*

4. **Dolomite crystals contain calcium magnesium carbonate, CaMg(CO$_3$)$_2$. Dolomite can be found, along with other substances, in dolostone, which is dug up for use in industry.**

   Draw lines to match each species to the type of substance.

   | dolostone | compound |
   | CaMg(CO$_3$)$_2$ | mineral |
   | dolomite | element |
   | calcium | rock |

   *(2 marks)*

5. **Decide whether each of the sentences below is talking about the Earth's core, the crust or the mantle. Tick the correct box for each.**

   |  | Core | Crust | Mantle |
   |---|---|---|---|
   | Scientists think it mainly consists of iron and one other element. | ☐ | ☐ | ☐ |
   | Mostly solid, but some parts do flow. | ☐ | ☐ | ☐ |
   | The layer which we live on. | ☐ | ☐ | ☐ |
   | Contains solid rocks and minerals. | ☐ | ☐ | ☐ |
   | Tectonic plates float on it. | ☐ | ☐ | ☐ |

   *(3 marks)*

6. **What causes earthquakes?**

   ......................................................................................................................................

   *(1 mark)*

   Score: /10

# Test 2: Rocks and the Rock Cycle

Give yourself **10 minutes** to do this test — there are **7 questions** to answer.

**Quick-fire Question**

1. What are fossils? Circle your answer.

    A   Compounds found in igneous rocks.

    B   Minerals formed from the remains of dead plants and animals.

    C   Rock fragments that have been exposed to heat and pressure.

    D   Salts left behind when water evaporates.

    *(1 mark)*

2. Which of the following are types of igneous rock? Circle your answers.

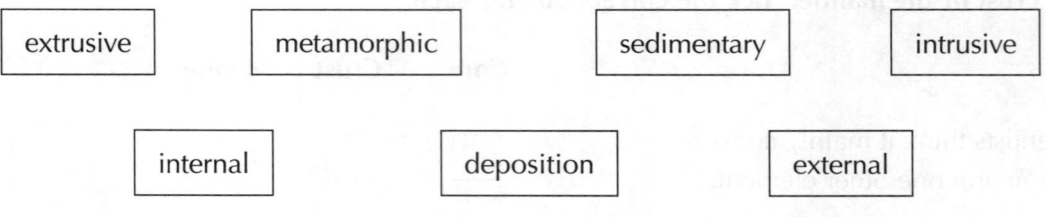

    *(1 mark)*

3. What name is given to melted underground rock?

    ..................................................................................................................................
    *(1 mark)*

4. A simplified part of the rock cycle is shown below. Fill in the gaps.

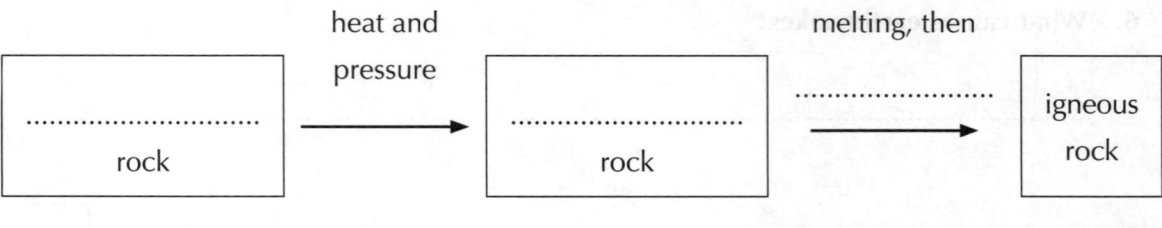

    *(2 marks)*

---

The Earth and the Atmosphere: Test 2

5. **A rock on a hillside is weathered and eroded until it breaks down into smaller pieces. Put the stages of the rock cycle below in the order that they will occur after this.**

   | transportation | exposure | deposition | compression | heat and pressure |

   1. ..........................................
   2. ..........................................
   3. ..........................................
   4. ..........................................
   5. ..........................................

   *(2 marks)*

6. **Give two causes of erosion.**

   ...................................................................................................................................
   *(1 mark)*

7. **Decide whether each of A-E describe igneous, metamorphic or sedimentary rocks. Write the letters in the correct columns of the table. Some letters may go in more than one column.**

   | A can contain layers | B can contain crystals | C formed from magma |

   | D relatively soft | E where fossils are most likely to be found |

   | Igneous | Metamorphic | Sedimentary |
   |---------|-------------|-------------|
   |         |             |             |

   *(2 marks)*

   Score: /10

# Test 3: Rocks and the Rock Cycle

Give yourself **10 minutes** to do this test — there are **8 questions** to answer.

**Quick-fire Question**

1. Which of the following are types of rock weathering? Circle your answer.

   A  Freeze-thaw          B  Onion skin

   C  Burial               D  Volcanic

   *(1 mark)*

2. Decide which type of igneous rock is being described by each of the statements below. Tick the correct box for each.

   |  | intrusive | extrusive |
   |---|---|---|
   | Formed underground. | ☐ | ☐ |
   | Formed when magma cools slowly. | ☐ | ☐ |
   | Contains small crystals. | ☐ | ☐ |

   *(2 marks)*

3. Complete the sentences below using some of the words given in the box.

   | composition | destroyed | age | metamorphic |
   |---|---|---|---|
   | layers | sedimentary | buried | crystals |

   .................................... rocks can contain fossils. These form when dead plants

   and animals sink to the sea floor and are .................................... by sediment.

   Over a long time, the .................................... of sediment are compressed,

   forming rock. Fossils can be used to work out the relative ....................................

   of a rock.

   *(2 marks)*

---

The Earth and the Atmosphere: Test 3

4. **Complete the sentences below by circling the correct answers in the brackets.**

   Eroded bits of rock are mostly carried away by water and ( **wind** / **people** ).

   This part of the rock cycle is called ( **transportation** / **deposition** ).
   
   *(1 mark)*

5. **What substance is removed from between sediment particles during compression?**

   ...................................................................................................................................
   
   *(1 mark)*

6. **What is meant by the term deposition?**

   ...................................................................................................................................

   ...................................................................................................................................
   
   *(1 mark)*

7. **What is uplift? Tick the correct box.**

   ☐ When a volcano erupts and releases igneous rocks into the air.

   ☐ When water pushes a sedimentary rock upwards.

   ☐ When sediments are transported through the air.

   ☐ When old rocks are pushed towards the surface by newer rocks.
   
   *(1 mark)*

8. **Give an example of a sedimentary rock.**

   ...................................................................................................................................
   
   *(1 mark)*

   Score: ☐ /10

# Test 4: Recycling

Give yourself **10 minutes** to do this test — there are **7 questions** to answer.

**Quick-fire Question**

1. What is a limited resource? Circle your answer.

   A   A resource that is necessary for our survival.

   B   A resource that has been recycled many times.

   C   A resource that will eventually run out.

   D   A resource that cannot be recycled.

*(1 mark)*

2. Give two examples of limited resources.

   1. ..................................................................................................................

   2. ..................................................................................................................
   *(2 marks)*

3. What is meant by recycling? Tick the correct box.

   ☐ Taking unwanted products and using the materials to make new products.

   ☐ Reusing a product many times before throwing it away.

   ☐ Extracting new materials from the Earth, but putting back as much as you take.

   ☐ Only using resources that won't run out any time soon.
   *(1 mark)*

4. Suggest one reason why recycling aluminium uses less energy than producing aluminium from scratch.

   ..................................................................................................................

   ..................................................................................................................
   *(1 mark)*

5. Some information about plastic bags is given in the table below.

| Made from: | crude oil |
|---|---|
| Production: | The crude oil is separated using fractional distillation, then a multi-step process is carried out to produce a polymer. The polymer is then used to make a plastic bag. |
| Disposal: | Taken to landfill, but doesn't break down (biodegrade). |

Use the information in the table to give two reasons why it would be better to recycle plastic bags to make new ones, rather than make new ones from scratch.

1. ...................................................................................................................

...................................................................................................................

2. ...................................................................................................................

...................................................................................................................
*(2 marks)*

6. **Complete the sentences below by circling the correct answers in the brackets.**

   Metals are extracted from metal ores, which must be mined out of the ground.

   This requires a lot of ( **energy** / **oxygen** ), which makes it an ( **expensive** / **inexpensive** )

   process. Recycling metals is usually much ( **less** / **more** ) cost-efficient than

   extracting metals from ores.

   *(2 marks)*

7. **Glass bottles can be recycled.**
   **Suggest why it is still better to reuse a glass bottle rather than recycle it.**

   ...................................................................................................................

   ...................................................................................................................
   *(1 mark)*

Score: /10

# Test 5: Carbon, the Atmosphere and Climate

Give yourself **10 minutes** to do this test — there are **7 questions** to answer.

**Quick-fire Question**

1. Which of the following reactions is carried out by all living things? Circle your answer.

   A   combustion         B   respiration

   C   photosynthesis     D   decomposition

   *(1 mark)*

2. Draw lines to match each gas to its percentage of the Earth's atmosphere.

   carbon dioxide        78%

   oxygen                21%

   nitrogen              0.04%

   *(1 mark)*

   Name another gas present in the atmosphere.

   ......................................................................................................................
   *(1 mark)*

3. Fill in the gaps to complete the equation for photosynthesis.

   water + .................... →(sunlight) oxygen + ....................

   *(2 marks)*

4. Give one way in which the climate has changed over the last hundred years.

   ......................................................................................................................
   *(1 mark)*

The Earth and the Atmosphere: Test 5

5. **Part of the carbon cycle is shown on the right.**

   Which arrow represents respiration?
   Write down the correct letter.

   ..................................................

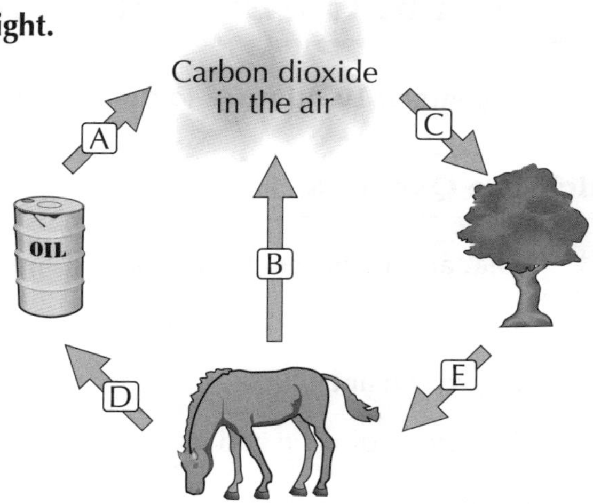

   *(1 mark)*

6. Complete the sentences below using some of the words given in the box.

   | Moon | atmosphere | oceans | warm |
   |---|---|---|---|
   | nitrogen | cool | Sun | carbon dioxide |

   Greenhouse gases, such as ................................................ , trap heat from

   the ................................ in the Earth's ................................ .

   This helps to keep the planet ................................ enough to support life.

   *(2 marks)*

7. **Fossil fuels are formed from the remains of organisms that died a long time ago. How is the carbon in fossil fuels returned to the air?**

   ..............................................................................................................................

   ..............................................................................................................................

   *(1 mark)*

   Score: /10

# Test 6: Carbon, the Atmosphere and Climate

Give yourself **10 minutes** to do this test — there are **7 questions** to answer.

**Quick-fire Question**

1. What are the products of photosynthesis? Circle your answer.

   A   carbon dioxide and water

   B   oxygen and glucose

   C   carbon dioxide and glucose

   D   water and oxygen

   *(1 mark)*

2. **Give two different human activities that increase the amount of carbon dioxide in the atmosphere.**

   1. ...........................................................................................................................................

   2. ...........................................................................................................................................
   *(2 marks)*

3. Complete the sentences below using the words given in the box.

   | respiration   combustion   photosynthesis |

   The carbon cycle shows the recycling of carbon through the environment.

   Carbon dioxide is removed from the air by ..................................... and the carbon

   is passed along the food chain when animals eat plants and other animals.

   ..................................... by plants and animals, and .....................................

   of fuels return carbon dioxide to the air, and the cycle starts again.

   *(1 mark)*

---

The Earth and the Atmosphere: Test 6     48     © CGP — not to be photocopied

4. An animal dies and is buried in the ground.
   Explain how the carbon in the animal remains is returned to the air.

   ..............................................................................................................................

   ..............................................................................................................................

   ..............................................................................................................................
   *(2 marks)*

5. Why does deforestation increase the amount of carbon dioxide in the atmosphere?

   ..............................................................................................................................

   ..............................................................................................................................
   *(1 mark)*

6. What two-word phrase is used to describe the change in the temperature of the Earth over the last hundred years? Tick the correct box.

   ☐ surface heating       ☐ Earth warming

   ☐ global greenhouse     ☐ global warming
   *(1 mark)*

7. Explain one potential effect of the change in the temperature of the Earth over the last hundred years.

   ..............................................................................................................................

   ..............................................................................................................................

   ..............................................................................................................................
   *(2 marks)*

Score: ☐ /10

# Mixed Questions

## Test 1: Mixed Questions

Give yourself **10 minutes** to do this test — there are **8 questions** to answer.

**Quick-fire Question**

1. What is magma? Circle your answer.

   A   The layer of the Earth between the core and the crust.

   B   Melted underground rock.

   C   A chemical compound that makes up rocks.

   D   A rock formed under high temperatures and pressures.

   *(1 mark)*

2. Luke pours some orange squash into a glass of water.
   The orange colour slowly spreads through the water.
   What is the name of this process?   Tick one box.

   ☐ Melting     ☐ Sublimation     ☐ Diffusion     ☐ Confusion

   *(1 mark)*

3. Aluminium oxide can be found in the Earth as the mineral corundum.
   Explain why carbon could not be used to extract aluminium from corundum.

   ..................................................................................................................................

   ..................................................................................................................................

   ..................................................................................................................................
   *(1 mark)*

4. Which of the following reactions is a combustion reaction?   Tick the correct box.

   ☐  $CuCO_3 \xrightarrow{heat} CuO + CO_2$

   ☐  $C_2H_4 + 3O_2 \rightarrow 2CO_2 + 2H_2O$

   ☐  $2NaOH + H_2SO_4 \rightarrow Na_2SO_4 + 2H_2O$

   *(1 mark)*

5. Decide whether each of the sentences below is true or false. Tick the correct box.

|  | True | False |
|---|---|---|
| Litmus paper gives you a value for pH. | ☐ | ☐ |
| Alkalis turn blue litmus paper red. | ☐ | ☐ |
| Pure water always has a neutral pH. | ☐ | ☐ |

*(2 marks)*

6. **Lithium and iodine can be combined to form a compound. Suggest what this compound is called.**

   .................................................................................................................................
   *(1 mark)*

7. **Draw the particle arrangements for the missing states of matter, and write in the missing label.**

   solid ........................ gas

   *(2 marks)*

8. **Complete the sentences below by circling the correct answers in the brackets.**

   Some metal oxides dissolve in water to form an ( **acidic / alkaline** ) solution.

   Some non-metal oxides dissolve in water to from an ( **acidic / alkaline** ) solution.
   *(1 mark)*

Score: /10

# Test 2: Mixed Questions

Give yourself **10 minutes** to do this test — there are **7 questions** to answer.

**Quick-fire Question**

1. Which of the following is in the correct size order, from smallest to largest?  Circle your answer.

   A   Elements → Compounds → Minerals → Rocks

   B   Minerals → Elements → Rocks → Compounds

   C   Compounds → Elements → Rocks → Minerals

   D   Elements → Minerals → Compounds → Rocks

   *(1 mark)*

2. A piece of zinc is added to a beaker of hydrochloric acid.  The beaker and its contents are weighed immediately, and then weighed again ten minutes later.  The mass is found to have decreased.  Which of the following is the reason for this?  Tick one box.

   ☐ The hydrogen gas produced has escaped.

   ☐ The carbon dioxide gas produced has escaped.

   ☐ The zinc atoms have been destroyed in the reaction.

   ☐ The zinc atoms have been converted into hydrogen atoms.

   *(1 mark)*

3. Hannah makes the following statement: "Hydrogen gas is a compound, because it is made of two atoms joined together."
   Explain why Hannah is wrong.

   ..................................................................................................................................

   ..................................................................................................................................

   ..................................................................................................................................

   *(1 mark)*

4. **Give two common advantages of recycling over making things from scratch.**

   1. ..............................................................................................................................

   2. ..............................................................................................................................
   *(2 marks)*

5. **Draw lines to match each rock type to how it is formed.**

   | sedimentary | Formed from rocks under heat and pressure. |
   
   | igneous | Formed from magma. |
   
   | metamorphic | Formed from layers of sediment. |
   
   *(1 mark)*

6. **Sodium is in the third row and the first column of the periodic table. What group and period is sodium in?**

   Group = ................................... Period = ...........................................
   *(1 mark)*

7. **Fill in the missing processes involved in changes of state.**

   A — ................................

   melting

   C — ........................

   B — ........................

   condensing

   *(3 marks)*

   Score: /10

# Test 3: Mixed Questions

Give yourself **10 minutes** to do this test — there are **6 questions** to answer.

**Quick-fire Question**

1. What is the chemical formula for sodium hydroxide? Circle your answer.

    A  NaOH

    B  SHO

    C  $HNO_3$

    D  $H_2SO_4$

    *(1 mark)*

2. Fibreglass consists of glass fibres embedded in plastic.
   What type of material is fibreglass?

   ..................................................................................................................................
   *(1 mark)*

   Fibreglass is used to make things like boats and skis.
   Suggest one property that fibreglass is likely to have.

   ..................................................................................................................................
   *(1 mark)*

3. The pie chart shows the proportions of gases that make up the Earth's atmosphere.
   Write labels for the gases that the letters A and B represent.

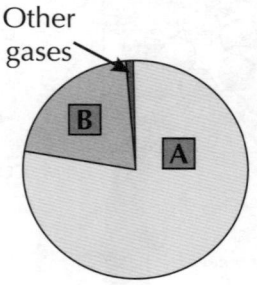

   A ........................................

   B ........................................

   *(2 marks)*

Mixed Questions: Test 3

4. Obsidian is a type of rock formed when magma cools too quickly for crystals to form. Suggest which type of rock obsidian is.

☐ Intrusive igneous  ☐ Sedimentary

☐ Extrusive igneous  ☐ Metamorphic

*(1 mark)*

5. Complete the sentences below by circling the correct answers in the brackets.

The elements in Group 7 are ( **metals** / **non-metals** ).

The elements in Group 7 get ( **more** / **less** ) reactive as you go down the group.

*(1 mark)*

6. Potassium sulfate is formed in the reaction between sulfuric acid and potassium hydroxide:

$$H_2SO_4 + 2KOH \rightarrow K_2SO_4 + 2H_2O$$

What would the pH of a potassium sulfate solution be?

.................................................................................................................................

*(1 mark)*

Draw lines to match each part of the equation with the most appropriate term.

| $H_2SO_4$ | salt |
| $KOH$ | acid |
| $K_2SO_4$ | water |
| $H_2O$ | alkali |

*(2 marks)*

Score: ☐ /10

# Test 4: Mixed Questions

Give yourself **10 minutes** to do this test — there are **7 questions** to answer.

**Quick-fire Question**

1. Which one of the following materials is magnetic? Circle your answer.

   A  Carbon

   B  Steel

   C  Bromine

   D  Gold

   *(1 mark)*

2. Only one of these equations is correctly balanced.
   Tick the box that shows the correctly balanced equation.

   ☐ $CuO + 2HCl \rightarrow CuCl_2 + H_2O$

   ☐ $Mg + HCl \rightarrow MgCl_2 + H_2$

   ☐ $CH_4 + O_2 \rightarrow CO_2 + 2H_2O$

   ☐ $3NaOH + 2H_2SO_4 \rightarrow Na_2SO_4 + 4H_2O$

   *(1 mark)*

3. Carbon dioxide can be dissolved in pure water to form a mixture.
   Which of the following would you NOT be able to separate out of the mixture without doing a chemical reaction? Circle all the answers that apply.

   $CO_2$         $H_2O$         $O_2$         $H_2$

   *(1 mark)*

4. Mirrors are usually made from a sheet of glass placed over a backing with a silver coating. Suggest one property of silver that makes it suitable for use in mirrors.

   ..............................................................................................................................

   *(1 mark)*

Mixed Questions: Test 4      56      © CGP — not to be photocopied

5. Give an example of a type of reaction that is endothermic.

   ..................................................................................................................................................
   *(1 mark)*

6. Decide whether each of A-F describe solids, liquids or gases.
   Write the letters in the correct columns of the table below.
   A letter may go in more than one column.

   | A Strong forces of attraction between particles. | B Weak forces of attraction between particles. |

   | C Match the shape of container. | D Can't be compressed. |

   | E Flow easily. | F Have a definite volume. |

   | Solids | Liquids | Gases |
   |---|---|---|
   |  |  |  |

   *(3 marks)*

7. Put the following steps for the formation of a metamorphic rock in order, from 1-5.
   The first one has been done for you.

   [ ] A. Compression and cementation of sediments form sedimentary rocks.

   [ ] B. Sediments are transported away from the original rock.

   [ ] C. Sediments are deposited and buried.

   [1] D. Exposed rocks are weathered and eroded.

   [ ] E. Rocks are further squashed and heated until they form metamorphic rocks.

   *(2 marks)*

   Score: ___ /10

# Test 5: Mixed Questions

Give yourself **10 minutes** to do this test — there are **7 questions** to answer.

**Quick-fire Question**

1. A solution has a pH of 9. Which of these terms describes the solution?
   Circle your answer.

   A  Strong acid     C  Strong alkali

   B  Weak acid       D  Weak alkali

   *(1 mark)*

2. Mei accidentally drops a sample of sand into a glass of water.
   Which of these methods would NOT be appropriate for retrieving the sand?
   Tick one box.

   ☐ Distillation        ☐ Filtration

   ☐ Chromatography      ☐ Evaporation

   *(1 mark)*

3. Complete the sentences below using the words given in the box.

   | quickly | slowly | large | small |

   Granite is an intrusive igneous rock. The magma that forms granite

   cools ........................ , which means ........................ crystals form.

   Basalt is an extrusive igneous rock. The magma that forms basalt

   cools ........................ , which means ........................ crystals form.

   *(2 marks)*

Mixed Questions: Test 5      58      © CGP — not to be photocopied

4. Which state of matter can be easily compressed? Circle the correct answer.

   solid     liquid     gas

   *(1 mark)*

5. Suggest two properties of metals which make them suitable for making aircraft.

   1. ..................................................................................................................................

   2. ..................................................................................................................................

   *(2 marks)*

6. A student carries out a chemical reaction between two reactants.
   The total mass of the products is 100 g. The mass of one of the reactants is 20 g.
   What is the mass of the other reactant?

   ..................................................................................................................................

   *(1 mark)*

7. A student is investigating the reaction between iron oxide and carbon.
   He writes down the unbalanced chemical equation for this reaction:

   $$Fe_2O_3 + C \rightarrow Fe + CO_2$$

   Write down the balanced equation for this reaction.

   ..................................................................................................................................

   *(1 mark)*

   Tick the box that completes the sentence:

   The iron oxide has been...

   ☐ reduced.    ☐ neutralised.    ☐ displaced.    ☐ oxidised.

   *(1 mark)*

   Score: /10

# Test 6: Mixed Questions

Give yourself **10 minutes** to do this test — there are **6 questions** to answer.

**Quick-fire Question**

1. What would you observe if you put a copper strip into a zinc sulfate solution? Circle your answer.

   A   Zinc would coat the copper strip.

   B   The solution would start to bubble.

   C   The copper strip would dissolve.

   D   You wouldn't observe any change.

   *(1 mark)*

2. Sulfur is a non-metal. Circle all of the properties that apply to sulfur.

   strong        low density

   high density        dull

   non-magnetic        shiny

   *(1 mark)*

3. Complete the sentences below using some of the words given in the box.

   | minimum | temperature | speeds up | slows down | changed | maximum |
   |---|---|---|---|---|---|

   A catalyst is a substance that ........................ a reaction,

   without being ........................ or used up in the reaction.

   Catalysts lower the ........................ amount of energy needed for a

   reaction to happen. This means a lower ........................ can be used

   to carry out the reaction.

   *(2 marks)*

Mixed Questions: Test 6

4. Decide whether each of the sentences below about the carbon cycle is true or false. Tick the correct box.

|  | True | False |
|---|---|---|
| Animals take in carbon dioxide and convert it to glucose. | ☐ | ☐ |
| Plants and algae respire to release energy. | ☐ | ☐ |
| When decomposers respire, carbon dioxide is released. | ☐ | ☐ |
| When fossil fuels are burned, they release oxygen into the atmosphere. | ☐ | ☐ |

*(2 marks)*

5. Give two properties of polymers that make them useful for making kayaks.

   1. ...........................................................................................................................

   2. ...........................................................................................................................

   *(2 marks)*

6. Complete the sentences below by circling the correct answers in the brackets.

   In a thermal decomposition reaction, a substance ( **breaks down** / **burns** )

   when it is ( **heated** / **cooled** ).

   The substance ( **reacts with nitrogen** / **does not react with anything**) and

   undergoes a ( **chemical** / **physical** ) change.

   *(2 marks)*

Score: /10

# Answers

**Classifying Materials: Test 1**

1. **A** *(1 mark)*

2. Solid — Density: **high**
   Liquid — Compressibility: **not easily squashed**
   Gas — Density: **low**
   Compressibility: **easily squashed**
   *(2 marks for all four correct, otherwise 1 mark for two or three correct.)*

3. There are **strong** forces of attraction between particles in a solid. The particles are held in a very **regular** arrangement. They **vibrate** to and fro in **fixed** positions.
   *(2 marks for all four correct, otherwise 1 mark for two or three correct.)*

4. In diffusion, particles move from an area of **higher** concentration to an area of **lower** concentration.
   *(1 mark for both correct.)*

5. A change of state is a physical change. — **True**
   A change of state involves a change in mass. — **False**
   A change of state involves a change in heat energy. — **True**
   *(2 marks for all three correct, otherwise 1 mark for two correct.)*

6. **D** — solid
   **A** — gas
   **B** — boiling point
   **C** — melting point
   *(2 marks for all four correct, otherwise 1 mark for two or three correct.)*

**Classifying Materials: Test 2**

1. **B** and **C** *(1 mark for both correct.)*

2. Condensing — When a gas turns into a liquid.
   Freezing — When a liquid turns into a solid.
   Boiling — When a liquid turns into a gas.
   Melting — When a solid turns into a liquid.
   *(1 mark for all four correct.)*

3. When a substance is heated, its particles **gain** energy. This makes the particles move more **quickly**, which **weakens** the forces of attraction between the particles.
   *(2 marks for all three correct, otherwise 1 mark for two correct.)*

4. Have a definite volume. — **solids** & **liquids**
   Are the shape of the container. — **liquids** & **gases**
   Flow easily. — **liquids** & **gases**
   *(2 marks for all six ticks correct, otherwise 1 mark for at least three ticks correct.)*

5. Gas pressure is caused by gas particles **colliding** with the inner walls of the container. Increasing the **temperature** makes the particles move faster. This means they hit the walls **harder** and more often. This **increases** the pressure.
   *(2 marks for all four correct, otherwise 1 mark for two or three correct.)*

6. There's a lot of space between gas particles *(1 mark)*, so they can be pushed closer together *(1 mark)*.

**Classifying Materials: Test 3**

1. **C** *(1 mark)*

2. Increase the temperature
   Decrease the volume
   *(1 mark for both correct.)*

3. **Cannot** be easily compressed.
   Particles are **free to move**.
   **Weak** forces of attraction between particles.
   *(2 marks for all three correct, otherwise 1 mark for two correct.)*

4. subliming *(1 mark)*

5.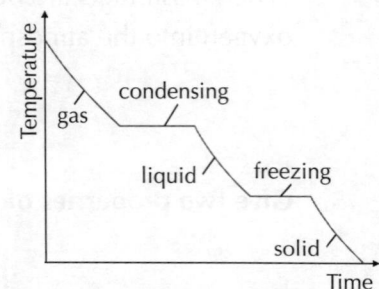

   *(3 marks — 1 mark for correct shape of curve, 1 mark for gas, liquid and solid labels all correct, 1 mark for condensing and freezing labels both correct.)*

6. When a balloon full of air is squeezed, the **volume** of the balloon decreases. This means that the **air particles** inside the balloon are squashed into a smaller space. The smaller the space becomes, the more the pressure **increases**. The balloon will eventually pop if the **pressure** increases too much.
   *(2 marks for all four correct, otherwise 1 mark for two or three correct.)*

## Classifying Materials: Test 4

1. **A**, **C**, **D** and **G**
   *(1 mark for all four correct.)*
2. All matter is made up of **atoms**. There are **many** types of atom. Each **element** contains only one type of atom. All **compounds** contain at least two types of atom bonded together.
   *(2 marks for all four correct, otherwise 1 mark for two or three correct.)*
3. **Water** — $H_2O$
   Carbon dioxide — **$CO_2$**
   **Sulfuric acid** — $H_2SO_4$
   Sodium chloride — **NaCl**
   *(2 marks for all four correct, otherwise 1 mark for two or three correct.)*
4. The chemicals you start with are called **reactants**.
   The chemicals you end up with are called **products**.
   *(1 mark for both correct.)*
5. 

   *(2 marks for all three correct, otherwise 1 mark for two correct.)*
6. Carbon: 5
   Hydrogen: 5
   Fluorine: 1
   Oxygen: 2
   *(2 marks for all four correct, otherwise 1 mark for two or three correct.)*

## Classifying Materials: Test 5

1. **C** *(1 mark)*
2. The elements in Group 1 are all metals. — **True**
   Group 1 elements are more reactive than Group 0 elements. — **True**
   Sodium is more reactive than caesium. — **False**
   All the Group 1 elements react with water. — **True**
   Potassium is more reactive than lithium. — **True**
   *(2 marks for all five correct, otherwise 1 mark for three or four correct.)*
3. A substance that contains only one type of atom *(1 mark)*.
4. Fe — Iron
   C — Carbon
   Cu — Copper
   Mg — Magnesium
   *(1 mark for all four correct.)*
5. E.g. the nitrogen atoms aren't bonded to the oxygen *(1 mark)*.
6. A — Compound
   B — Mixture
   C — Element
   D — Mixture
   *(2 marks for all four correct, otherwise 1 mark for two or three correct.)*
7. sodium + chlorine $\rightarrow$ sodium **chloride** *(1 mark)*
   2**Na** + $Cl_2$ $\rightarrow$ 2**NaCl** *(1 mark)*

## Classifying Materials: Test 6

1. **C** *(1 mark)*
2. The insoluble substance can be removed from the mixture by **filtration**.
   The soluble substance can be separated from the water by **evaporation**.
   *(1 mark for both correct.)*
3. 140 g *(1 mark)*
4. **A** *(1 mark)*
5. Solute — The solid being dissolved.
   Solution — A mixture of a solute and a solvent.
   Saturated — A solution where no more solid will dissolve at that temperature.
   Solubility — A measure of how much solute will dissolve.
   Insoluble — Will not dissolve.
   *(3 marks for all five correct, otherwise 2 marks for three correct, or 1 mark for one or two correct.)*
6. A pure substance can be made up of one type of compound. — **True**
   The molecules in pure substances can be separated using physical methods. — **False**
   Air is a mixture of different gases. — **True**
   A mixture contains different substances which aren't chemically combined. — **True**
   *(2 marks for all four correct, otherwise 1 mark for two or three correct.)*
7. The water sample must be impure (because pure water boils at 100° C) *(1 mark)*.

## Classifying Materials: Test 7

1. **B** *(1 mark)*
2. 1 — The rock salt is ground up with a pestle and mortar.
   2 — The rock salt is added to water and stirred until the salt has dissolved.
   3 — The mixture is filtered with a funnel and filter paper.
   4 — The mixture is heated until the water has evaporated.
   *(2 marks for all four correct, otherwise 1 mark for two correct.)*
3. insoluble *(1 mark)*
4. The water will evaporate into the air and be lost *(1 mark)*.
5. When you add a solute to a **solvent**, the **bonds** holding the solute particles together sometimes break. The **solute** particles then mix with the particles in the liquid forming a **solution**. This is called **dissolving**.
   *(2 marks for all five correct, otherwise 1 mark for three or four correct.)*
6. Liquid C *(1 mark)*
7. a chromatogram *(1 mark)*
8. Solvent, Beaker, Filter paper *(1 mark for all three correct.)*

## Classifying Materials: Test 8

1. **B** *(1 mark)*
2. 1 — Draw a pencil line near the bottom of a piece of chromatography paper.
   2 — Put spots of ink along the pencil line.
   3 — Roll up the paper.
   4 — Put the paper into a beaker containing a small amount of solvent.
   5 — Wait for the solvent to seep up the paper.
   6 — Remove the paper from the solvent.
   7 — Unroll the paper.
   *(3 marks for all six correct, otherwise 2 marks for four correct, or 1 mark for two or three correct.)*

3. a solution, a mixture *(1 mark for both correct.)*
4. B and D *(1 mark for both correct.)*
5. In **fractional** distillation, a flask containing different liquids is **heated** and the liquid that boils at the **lowest** temperature evaporates first. The vapour is then **cooled** until it condenses and is collected.
   *(2 marks for all four correct, otherwise 1 mark for two or three correct.)*
6. A — Thermometer
   B — Water out
   C — Condenser
   D — (Round-bottomed) flask
   E — (Ink and water) mixture
   F — (Pure distilled) water
   *(2 marks for all six correct, otherwise 1 mark for at least three correct.)*

## Classifying Materials: Test 9

1. **D** *(1 mark)*
2. A material that contains a combination of metals is called an **alloy**. Adding **iron** to a material will make it magnetic.
   *(1 mark for both correct.)*
3. brittle and can shatter easily — **Non-metals**
   have high densities — **Metals**
   good insulators of electricity — **Non-metals**
   poor conductors of heat — **Non-metals**
   high melting and boiling points — **Metals**
   shiny when polished — **Metals**
   *(2 marks for all six correct, otherwise 1 mark for at least three correct.)*
4. It means that the vibrations of hot particles are easily passed on through the metal. *(1 mark)*

5. Polymers — Substances made up of long chains of molecules.
   Ceramics — Stiff and brittle materials made by baking substances like clay.
   Composites — Materials made up of two or more materials together.
   *(1 mark for all three correct.)*
6. E.g. the pot is made from metal because metal is a good conductor of heat *(1 mark)*, so the heat can pass through the pan and cook the food inside *(1 mark)*. The handles are plastic because plastic is a poor conductor of heat *(1 mark)*, so you can pick up the pot by the handles without getting burned *(1 mark)*.

## Classifying Materials: Test 10

1. **C** *(1 mark)*
2. All metals are magnetic. — **False**
   All non-metals are non-magnetic. — **True**
   Electrical wires are made of metal. — **True**
   All non-metals are gases. — **False**
   *(2 marks for all four correct, otherwise 1 mark for two or three correct.)*
3. High tensile strength — Can be pulled hard without breaking.
   Malleable — Easily shaped.
   Ductile — Can be drawn into a wire.
   Sonorous — Makes a sound when hit.
   *(2 marks for all four correct, otherwise 1 mark for two correct.)*
4. Graphite isn't hard-wearing, so its particles are easily scrubbed away. *(1 mark)*
5. electrons *(1 mark)*
6. **Polymers** — can be flexible,
   **Ceramics** — always brittle, always stiff,
   **Both** — electrical insulator, heat insulator
   *(3 marks for all five correct, otherwise 2 marks for four correct or 1 mark for three correct.)*

## Chemical Changes: Test 1

1. **A** and **D**
   *(1 mark for both correct.)*

2. $CH_4 + 2O_2 \rightarrow CO_2 + 2H_2O$
   *(1 mark for both numbers correct.)*

3. In an exothermic reaction, energy is **given out to** the surroundings. This is usually shown by **an increase** in the temperature of the reaction mixture.
   In an endothermic reaction, energy is **taken in from** the surroundings. This is usually shown by **a decrease** in the temperature of the reaction mixture.
   *(2 marks for all four correct, otherwise 1 mark for two correct.)*

4. Combustion — When a substance burns in the air to release energy.
   Decomposition — When a substance breaks down to form new substances.
   Oxidation — When a substance combines with oxygen.
   *(2 mark for all three correct, otherwise 1 mark for one correct.)*

5. oxygen, fuel, heat
   *(3 marks — 1 mark for each correct answer.)*

6. A substance that speeds up a reaction without being changed/used up *(1 mark)*.

## Chemical Changes: Test 2

1. **C** *(1 mark)*

2. The mass would decrease *(1 mark)*.

3. Propane is a hydrocarbon. When propane is burned in a good supply of air, a **combustion** reaction takes place. The reaction gives out energy in the form of **heat**, which means it is **exothermic**. The reaction also gives out energy in the form of **light**.
   *(2 marks for all four correct, otherwise 1 mark for two or three correct.)*

4. iron + oxygen → iron oxide *(1 mark)*

5. carbon dioxide, water
   *(1 mark for both correct.)*

6. E.g. for each type of atom on the left-hand side of the equation, there is the same number of that type of atom on the right-hand side of the equation *(1 mark)*.

7. E.g. more bubbles will be seen in the flask containing the catalyst *(1 mark)*, because the catalyst will speed up the reaction *(1 mark)*.

## Chemical Changes: Test 3

1. **C** *(1 mark)*

2. sodium + water → sodium hydroxide + hydrogen *(1 mark)*

3. Endothermic, because e.g. the pack cools the surroundings/injury *(1 mark)*.

4. They lower the minimum amount of energy required for the reaction to happen *(1 mark)*.

5. $2CuO + C \rightarrow 2Cu + CO_2$
   *(1 mark for correct equation, 1 mark for correct balancing.)*

6. **B** *(1 mark)*

7. Any two from: e.g. they could cost the company a lot of money. / Different catalysts will be needed for different reactions. / They will need to be cleaned. / They could become poisoned by impurities.
   *(2 marks — 1 mark for each sensible answer.)*

8. oxidation *(1 mark)*

## Chemical Changes: Test 4

1. **B** *(1 mark)*

2. sodium hydroxide solution — pH 13
   sulfuric acid — pH 1
   pure water — pH 7
   *(1 mark for all three correct.)*

3. E.g. a dye that changes colour depending on the pH *(1 mark)*.

4. Magda has a solution of potassium hydroxide. This solution is **alkaline**. She adds some nitric acid to the solution. Adding the acid makes the pH of the solution **decrease**. After she has added the acid, the solution contains **a salt**.
   *(2 marks for all three correct, otherwise 1 mark for two correct.)*

5. 

| Indicator | Colour at pH 6 | Colour at pH 14 |
|---|---|---|
| Universal Indicator | yellow | **blue / purple** |
| Litmus Paper | **red** | blue |

*(2 marks — 1 mark for each correct answer.)*

6. E.g. remove a small sample after every few drops and check the pH using Universal indicator *(1 mark)*. The pH will be 7 / the indicator will turn green when enough acid has been added *(1 mark)*.
   Tallulah could use sulfuric acid instead of hydrochloric acid *(1 mark)*.

## Chemical Changes: Test 5

1. **D** (1 mark)

2. The solution would turn yellow (1 mark).

3. Acid + Alkali → Salt + Water (1 mark)

4. The pH of the strongest acid is **0**. The pH of the strongest alkali is **14**. The pH of a neutral solution is **7**. (3 marks — 1 mark for each correct answer.)

5.

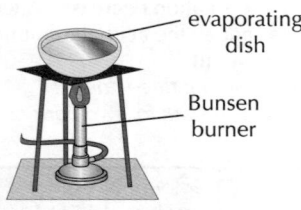

evaporating dish
Bunsen burner

(1 mark)

6. neutralisation (1 mark) potassium nitrate (1 mark)

7. E.g. Universal indicator can be used to obtain a value for the pH, whereas litmus paper can't. / Universal indicator tells you the strength of the acid or alkali, whereas litmus paper doesn't (1 mark).

## Chemical Changes: Test 6

1. **C** (1 mark)

2. Some metals, such as **gold** are so **unreactive** that they are found in the Earth in their pure form. Other metals are mostly found in the Earth as metal **oxides** and have to be extracted from **ores**.
(2 marks for all four correct, otherwise 1 mark for two or three correct).

3.

|    | $ZnSO_4$ | KCl | $Pb(NO_3)_2$ |
|----|----------|-----|--------------|
| Mg | ✓        | ✗   | ✓            |
| Fe | ✗        | ✗   | ✓            |

(1 mark for all three correct.)

4. Most soluble non-metal oxides form acidic solutions. — **True**
Metals below hydrogen in the reactivity series will react with acids. — **False**
Insoluble metal oxides can be used to neutralise acids. — **True**
(2 marks for all three correct, otherwise 1 mark for two correct).

5. copper, hydrogen, zinc, carbon, calcium, sodium
(2 marks for all six in the correct order, otherwise 1 mark for at least four in the correct order.)

6. E.g. both reactions will produce bubbles (1 mark). The reaction with magnesium will produce more bubbles / will bubble faster than the reaction with iron (1 mark).

## Chemical Changes: Test 7

1. **A** (1 mark)

2. A rock that contains metal or metal compounds (1 mark).

3. Can be extracted using carbon: zinc, iron
Can't be extracted using carbon: aluminium, magnesium
(1 mark for all correct.)

4. electrolysis (1 mark)

5. Hold a lit splint to the open end of the test tube (1 mark). If the test tube contains hydrogen, there will be a (squeaky) pop (1 mark).

6. From least reactive to most reactive: Z, X, Y
(1 mark for all three in the correct order.)

7. E.g. basic/form alkaline solutions / solid at room temperature / react with acids.
(2 marks — 1 mark for each correct answer.)

8. phosphorus, silicon, nitrogen (1 mark for all three correct.)

## Chemical Changes: Test 8

1. **B** (1 mark)

2. gas at room temperature, reacts with alkalis in solution (1 mark for both correct.)

3. hydrochloric acid + zinc → **zinc chloride** + **hydrogen**
(2 marks — 1 mark for each correct product.)

4. e.g. gold / silver (1 mark)

5. Iron is a useful metal that must be extracted from its ore, iron oxide. In order to do this, iron oxide is mixed with a fuel called coke and heated to a **high** temperature in a blast **furnace**. The coke contains **carbon**, which **reduces** the iron oxide to produce iron.
(2 marks for all four correct, otherwise 1 mark for two or three correct.)

6. copper (1 mark)
The iron has displaced the copper from the copper nitrate solution (to form green iron sulfate solution and solid copper metal) (1 mark), because iron is more reactive than copper (1 mark).

**The Earth and the Atmosphere: Test 1**

1. **A** *(1 mark)*
2.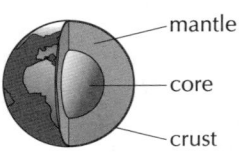
   — mantle
   — core
   — crust
   *(1 mark for all three correct.)*
3. The **surface** of the planet is broken into several large pieces called **tectonic plates**, which move around very **slowly**. **Volcanoes** can occur where two of the pieces meet.
   *(2 marks for all four correct, otherwise 1 mark for two or three correct.)*
4. dolostone — rock
   $CaMg(CO_3)_2$ — compound
   dolomite — mineral
   calcium — element
   *(2 marks for all four correct, otherwise 1 mark for two correct.)*
5. Scientists think it mainly consists of iron and one other element. — **Core**
   Mostly solid, but some parts do flow. — **Mantle**
   The layer which we live on. — **Crust**
   Contains solid rocks and minerals. — **Crust**
   Tectonic plates float on it. — **Mantle**
   *(3 marks for all five correct, otherwise 2 marks for four correct or 1 mark for two or three correct.)*
6. E.g. tectonic plates moving very suddenly *(1 mark)*.

**The Earth and the Atmosphere: Test 2**

1. **B** *(1 mark)*
2. extrusive, intrusive
   *(1 mark for both correct.)*
3. magma *(1 mark)*
4. **sedimentary** rock
   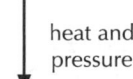
   heat and pressure
   **metamorphic** rock
   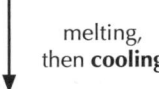
   melting, then **cooling**
   igneous rock
   *(2 marks — 1 mark for sedimentary and metamorphic the correct way around, 1 mark for cooling.)*
5. 1. transportation
   2. deposition
   3. compression
   4. heat and pressure
   5. exposure
   *(2 marks for all five in the correct order, otherwise 1 mark for four in the correct order.)*
6. Any two from: e.g. wind / waves / rain
   *(1 mark for two correct answers.)*
7. Igneous — B, C
   metamorphic — A, B
   Sedimentary — A, D, E
   *(2 marks for all letters in the correct columns, otherwise 1 mark for three or four letters in the correct columns.)*

**The Earth and the Atmosphere: Test 3**

1. **A** and **B**
   *(1 mark for both correct.)*
2. Formed underground. — **intrusive**
   Formed when magma cools slowly. — **intrusive**
   Contains small crystals. — **extrusive**
   *(2 marks for all three correct, otherwise 1 mark for two correct.)*
3. **Sedimentary** rocks can contain fossils. These form when dead plants and animals sink to the sea floor and are **buried** by sediment. Over a long time, the **layers** of sediment are compressed, forming rock. Fossils can be used to work out the relative **age** of a rock.
   *(2 marks for all four correct, otherwise 1 mark for two or three correct.)*
4. Eroded bits of rock are mostly carried away by water and **wind**. This part of the rock cycle is called **transportation**.
   *(1 mark for both correct.)*
5. water *(1 mark)*
6. E.g. the laying down of sediment. / When sediment sinks to the bottom of lakes/seas *(1 mark)*.
7. When old rocks are pushed towards the surface by newer rocks *(1 mark)*.
8. e.g. sandstone *(1 mark)*

## The Earth and the Atmosphere: Test 4

1. **C** (1 mark)
2. e.g. metal ores, fossil fuels (2 marks — 1 mark for each sensible answer.)
3. Taking unwanted products and using the materials to make new products (1 mark).
4. E.g. the aluminium doesn't have to be mined out of the ground / extracted from its ore (which requires a lot of energy) (1 mark).
5. E.g. recycling uses up less crude oil, which is a limited resource (1 mark). Recycling means that fewer plastic bags will go to landfill (1 mark).
6. Metals are produced from metal **ores**, which must be mined out of the ground. This requires a lot of **energy**, which makes it an **expensive** process. Recycling metals is usually much **more** cost-efficient than extracting metals from ores. (2 marks for all four correct, otherwise 1 mark for two or three correct.)
7. E.g. reusing the glass bottle requires even less energy than recycling it (1 mark).

## The Earth and the Atmosphere: Test 5

1. **B** (1 mark)
2. carbon dioxide — 0.04%
   oxygen — 21%
   nitrogen — 78%
   (1 mark for all three correct.)
   e.g. water vapour / argon (1 mark)
3. water + **carbon dioxide** → oxygen + **glucose**
   (2 marks — 1 mark for each correct compound.)
4. E.g. the temperature of the planet has increased. / Rainfall patterns have changed (1 mark).
5. **B** (1 mark)

6. Greenhouse gases, such as **carbon dioxide**, trap heat from the **Sun** in the Earth's **atmosphere**. This helps to keep the planet **warm** enough to support life.
(2 marks for all four correct, otherwise 1 mark for two or three correct.)
7. The fossil fuels are burned and carbon dioxide is given off (1 mark).

## The Earth and the Atmosphere: Test 6

1. **B** (1 mark)
2. e.g. burning fossil fuels, deforestation (2 marks — 1 mark for each sensible answer.)
3. The carbon cycle shows the recycling of carbon through the environment. Carbon dioxide is removed from the air by **photosynthesis** and the carbon is passed along the food chain when animals eat plants and other animals. **Respiration** by plants and animals, and **combustion** of fuels return carbon dioxide to the air, and the cycle starts again.
(1 mark for all three correct.)
4. E.g. decomposers/bacteria feed on the remains (1 mark). When the decomposers/bacteria respire, they release carbon dioxide back into the air (1 mark). / The animal remains eventually form fossil fuels (1 mark). When the fossil fuels are burned, carbon dioxide is realised back in to the air (1 mark).
5. E.g. fewer trees means less carbon dioxide is removed from the atmosphere by photosynthesis (1 mark).
6. global warming (1 mark)
7. E.g. more flooding (1 mark), due to glaciers melting (1 mark). / Difficulties producing crops (1 mark), due to changing rainfall patterns (1 mark).

## Mixed Questions: Test 1

1. **B** (1 mark)
2. Diffusion (1 mark)
3. Aluminium is more reactive than carbon. Carbon can only be used to extract metals that are less reactive than itself (1 mark).
4. $C_2H_4 + 3O_2 \rightarrow 2CO_2 + 2H_2O$ (1 mark)
5. Litmus paper gives you a value for pH. — **False**
   Alkalis turn blue litmus paper red. — **False**
   Pure water always has a neutral pH. — **True**
   (2 marks for all three correct, otherwise 1 mark for two correct.)
6. lithium iodide (1 mark)
7.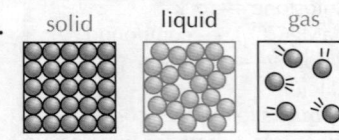
   (2 marks for all three correct, otherwise 1 mark for two correct.)
8. Some metal oxides dissolve in water to form an **alkaline** solution. Some non-metal oxides dissolve in water to form an **acidic** solution.
(1 mark for both correct.)

## Mixed Questions: Test 2

1. **A** (1 mark)
2. The hydrogen gas produced has escaped. (1 mark)
3. E.g. Hannah is wrong because hydrogen gas contains only one type of atom, so it is an element. (Compounds must contain two or more different elements.) (1 mark)
4. Any two from: e.g. it uses less of Earth's limited resources. / It uses less energy. / It saves money. / It makes less rubbish.
(2 marks — 1 mark for each sensible answer.)
5. sedimentary — Formed from layers of sediment.
igneous — Formed from magma.
metamorphic — Formed from rocks under heat and pressure.
(1 mark for all three correct.)
6. Group = 1
Period = 3
(1 mark for both correct.)
7. A — subliming
B — freezing
C — boiling
(3 marks — 1 mark for each correct answer.)

## Mixed Questions: Test 3

1. **A** (1 mark)
2. a composite (1 mark)
e.g. low density / strong (1 mark)
3. A — nitrogen
B — oxygen
(2 marks — 1 mark for each correct answer.)
4. Extrusive igneous (1 mark)
5. The elements in Group 7 are **non-metals**. The elements in Group 7 get **less** reactive as you go down the group.
(1 mark for both correct.)
6. 7 (1 mark)
$H_2SO_4$ — acid
KOH — alkali
$K_2SO_4$ — salt
$H_2O$ — water
(2 marks for all four correct, otherwise 1 mark for two correct.)

## Mixed Questions: Test 4

1. **B** (1 mark)
2. $CuO + 2HCl \rightarrow CuCl_2 + H_2O$ (1 mark)
3. $O_2$ and $H_2$ (1 mark for both correct.)
4. E.g. silver is shiny/reflective when polished (1 mark).
5. e.g. thermal decomposition (1 mark)
6. Solids — A, D, F
Liquids — B, C, D, E, F
Gases — B, C, E
(3 marks — 1 mark for each correct column.)
7. 1 — D, 2 — B, 3 — C, 4 — A, 5 — E,
(2 marks for all steps in the correct order, otherwise 1 mark for at least three steps in the correct order.)

## Mixed Questions: Test 5

1. **D** (1 mark)
2. Chromatography (1 mark)
3. Granite is an intrusive igneous rock. The magma that forms granite cools **slowly**, which means **large** crystals form. Basalt is an extrusive igneous rock. The magma that forms basalt cools **quickly**, which means **small** crystals form.
(2 marks for all four correct, otherwise 1 mark for two or three correct.)
4. gas (1 mark)
5. Any two from: e.g. strong / malleable / high melting point.
(2 marks — 1 mark for each sensible answer.)
6. 100 − 20 = **80 g** (1 mark)
7. $2Fe_2O_3 + 3C \rightarrow 4Fe + 3CO_2$ (1 mark)
reduced. (1 mark)

## Mixed Questions: Test 6

1. **D** (1 mark)
2. non-magnetic, low density, dull
(1 mark for all three correct.)
3. A catalyst is a substance that **speeds up** a reaction, without being **changed** or used up in the reaction. Catalysts lower the **minimum** amount of energy needed for a reaction to happen. This means a lower **temperature** can be used to carry out the reaction.
(2 marks for all four correct, otherwise 1 mark for two or three correct.)
4. Animals take in carbon dioxide and covert it to glucose. — **False**
Plants and algae respire to release energy. — **True**
When decomposers respire, carbon dioxide is released. — **True**
When fossil fuels are burned, they release oxygen into the atmosphere. — **False**
(2 marks for all four correct, otherwise 1 mark for two or three correct.)
5. Any two from: e.g. they are easily moulded into shape. / They have a low density. / Many of them are waterproof. / They're lightweight. / They're strong.
(2 marks — 1 mark for each sensible answer.)
6. In a thermal decomposition reaction, a substance **breaks down** when it is **heated**. The substance **does not react with anything** and undergoes a **chemical** change.
(2 marks for all four correct, otherwise 1 mark for two or three correct.)

# Progress Charts

When you've completed and marked a test,
stick your score in the correct place on these charts.

### Classifying Materials

|  |  |
|---|---|
| Test 1 | / 10 |
| Test 2 | / 10 |
| Test 3 | / 10 |
| Test 4 | / 10 |
| Test 5 | / 10 |
| Test 6 | / 10 |
| Test 7 | / 10 |
| Test 8 | / 10 |
| Test 9 | / 10 |
| Test 10 | / 10 |

### The Earth and the Atmosphere

|  |  |
|---|---|
| Test 1 | / 10 |
| Test 2 | / 10 |
| Test 3 | / 10 |
| Test 4 | / 10 |
| Test 5 | / 10 |
| Test 6 | / 10 |

### Chemical Changes

|  |  |
|---|---|
| Test 1 | / 10 |
| Test 2 | / 10 |
| Test 3 | / 10 |
| Test 4 | / 10 |
| Test 5 | / 10 |
| Test 6 | / 10 |
| Test 7 | / 10 |
| Test 8 | / 10 |

### Mixed Questions

|  |  |
|---|---|
| Test 1 | / 10 |
| Test 2 | / 10 |
| Test 3 | / 10 |
| Test 4 | / 10 |
| Test 5 | / 10 |
| Test 6 | / 10 |

Once you've filled in your score, use the table below for some advice on what to try next.

| Score | |
|---|---|
| 0-4 | You're not quite there yet — keep revising the topics in this test and look where you're going wrong, then have another go at the same test. |
| 5-8 | You're doing really well — make sure you keep revising the topics in this test, then take another test to try and improve your score. |
| 9-10 | You've aced this test — well done! Take a well-earned break then have a go at another test. After all, practice makes perfect... |